THE
HOPE
OF
Lent

DAILY
REFLECTIONS
FROM
Pope
Francis

Diane M. Houdek

franciscan
media

Cover and book design by Mark Sullivan
Cover image © iStock | nkbimages

Library of Congress Cataloging-in-Publication Data
Names: Francis, Pope, 1936- author. | Houdek, Diane M., compiler.
Title: The hope of Lent : daily reflections from Pope Francis / Diane M. Houdek.
Description: Cincinnati : Franciscan Media, 2017. | Includes bibliographical references.
Identifiers: LCCN 2016047426 | ISBN 9781632531605 (trade paper)
Subjects: LCSH: Lent—Prayers and devotions. | Catholic Church—Prayers and devotions. | Common lectionary (1992)
Classification: LCC BX2170.L4 F72813 2017 | DDC 242/.34—dc23

LC record available at https://lccn.loc.gov/2016047426

ISBN 978-1-63253-160-5

Published by Franciscan Media
28 W. Liberty St.
Cincinnati, OH 45202
www.FranciscanMedia.org

Printed in the United States of America.
Printed on acid-free paper.
17 18 19 20 21 5 4 3 2 1

CONTENTS

INTRODUCTION
Hope in God's Merciful Love

*W*e might think that the hope of Lent has to do with our hope that we will get through it, that we will come to the end of it. We see Lent as an obstacle course we need to navigate in order to get to the great feast of Easter. But while the Lenten season is indeed preparation for our Easter celebration, the hope of this season is that we will find our lives transformed by the many ways we encounter God's Word, by the richness of the Scripture readings chosen to encourage, to challenge, to confront, to comfort. Focusing only on the end goal would cause us to miss so much along the way.

The greatest hope of Lent is the discovery that it's not only about penance, deprivation, spiritual struggles, and rooting out sin in our lives. Those are often the things *we* do during Lent. But the hope of Lent lies in what God does. From the beginning of his pontificate, Pope Francis has made mercy his hallmark. It's no surprise that he declared a special year dedicated to the contemplation of mercy. Pope Francis wants us to realize that God's mercy and grace surround us not just in special times and places but always and everywhere. Lent is a time to discover the extraordinary in the ordinary, to be surprised by God's mercy when we least expect it.

As the season begins, think about the hopes you have for Lent this year. Think about what changes you want to see in your life, in the world. Let the words of Pope Francis guide you on a journey of bringing those hopes to fulfillment.

ASH WEDNESDAY
Be Faithful to the Gospel
JOEL 2:12–18; 2 CORINTHIANS 5:20—6:2; MATTHEW 6:1–6, 16–18

A WORD FROM POPE FRANCIS

*W*ith its invitations to conversion, Lent comes providentially to awaken us, to rouse us from torpor, from the risk of moving forward by inertia. The exhortation which the Lord addresses to us through the prophet Joel is strong and clear: "Return to me with all your heart" (Joel 2:12). Why must we return to God? Because something is not right in us, not right in society, in the Church and we need to change, to give it a new direction. And this is called needing to convert! Once again Lent comes to make its prophetic appeal, to remind us that it is possible to create something new within ourselves and around us, simply because God is faithful, always faithful, for he cannot deny himself, he continues to be rich in goodness and mercy, and he is always ready to forgive and start afresh.

TAKING THE WORD TO HEART

People often remark on the way our churches are filled on Ash Wednesday. It's not a holy day of obligation. No one is required to attend Mass or receive blessed ashes. But there's something about the beginning of this season of Lent that draws us in, calls us to return to sanity, to a bit of austerity, to a change of heart and mind. It's a second chance at our new year's resolutions, long since broken and forgotten. It's a second chance at making changes in our lives. For some people, it's no less than a second chance at life. That something that draws us is God's grace. And it's drawing us back to God's merciful embrace.

There's something attractive about Lent beginning in the middle of an ordinary week, catching us in the midst of our daily occupations and asking us to take time out to find God there. Lent doesn't take us away from our ordinary lives, but rather it invites us to bring a new and holy attention to those activities. This should be the way with all of our spiritual practices. We take time apart in order to return to our daily activities with new inspiration. God will always surprise us with possibilities when we least expect them. Let this Lent be one of those surprises.

BRINGING THE WORD TO LIFE

The prophet Joel calls for a public ritual of repentance. Jesus reminds his followers that our deepest need is between ourselves and the Father. Both are necessary. Which do you need this Lent?

How might your Lenten observances contain a healthy balance of public and private prayer? Choose something this Lent that will enhance your day-to-day interactions with the people in your life.

POPE FRANCIS PRAYS

In the face of so many wounds that hurt us
and could harden our hearts,
we are called to dive into the sea of prayer,
which is the sea of God's boundless love,
to taste his tenderness.

THURSDAY AFTER ASH WEDNESDAY
Stop and Choose
DEUTERONOMY 30:15–20; LUKE 9:22–25

A WORD FROM POPE FRANCIS

Today the Church tells us: "You are responsible; you have to choose." We live in a rush, we are on the run, without noticing what the path is like; and we let ourselves be carried along by the needs, by the necessities of the days, but without thinking. It will do us good to stop for a bit—five, ten minutes—and ask ourselves the question: What is the speed of my life? Do I reflect on my actions? How is my relationship with God and with my family?

Today, at the moment in which we stop to think about these things and to make decisions, to choose something, we know that the Lord is with us, is beside us, to help us. He never lets us go alone. He is always with us. Even in the moment of choosing. Because it takes a bit of courage to stop and ask myself: "How do I stand before God, how are my relationships in the family, what do I need to change, what should I choose?"

TAKING THE WORD TO HEART

Moses tells the people: "I set before you life and death. Choose life." It's easy to slide past this question by framing it in terms of the big, obvious issues: murder, abortion, the death penalty, war, euthanasia. We feel confident, perhaps even a bit smug, that of course we choose life. We might even be pleased with the fact that we have created a "good life" for ourselves and our families— successful, affluent, self-sufficient.

But Pope Francis reminds us that there are subtler ways in which we fail to make choices that tend toward life rather than death. We might be so busy making a good living that we miss living a good life. We might be active volunteers in our parish and community but neglect our children—or even our prayer life!— because of the pressure of too many meetings. We might be so busy taking care of others that we let our own health and well-being suffer. We know that we could all take better care of our bodies, minds, and spirits.

Lent bursts into our lives each year to give us the opportunity to ask the hard questions. And we ask them in the context of prayer, of time spent with God. As the pope reminds us, God will give us the grace and courage to ask—and answer—the challenging questions.

BRINGING THE WORD TO LIFE

In so many ways, different for each of us, the choice between life and death is still a choice we have to make. Perhaps this is what it means to take up our cross. If we're honest with ourselves, we probably know what that choice involves at this point in time. Make a commitment today to take that step toward life. You might want to share it with a trusted friend who can hold you accountable.

POPE FRANCIS PRAYS

Let us have faith in this Lord, who is with us,
and when He tells us: choose between good and evil
He helps us to choose good.
Let us ask him for the grace to be courageous.

FRIDAY AFTER ASH WEDNESDAY
Abstaining from Injustice
ISAIAH 58:1–9A; MATTHEW 9:14–15

*T*A WORD FROM POPE FRANCIS
oday is Friday, I can't eat meat. I'll make myself a nice plate of seafood, a nice banquet.... I'm observing it, I'm not eating meat." But this way amounts to sins of gluttony. This is the distinction between formal and real that is spoken of in the First Reading from the Book of the Prophet Isaiah (58:1–9a). I cannot say: I fulfill the first three Commandments...and more or less the others. No, they are joined: love for God and love for one's neighbor are joined and if you want to do real, not formal, penance, you must do it before God and also with your brother, with your neighbor.

Unfortunately, so many men and women have faith, but split the Tablets of the Law. You cannot make offerings to the Church on the shoulders of injustice perpetrated against your employees. One who does not do justice with the people who are dependent on him is not a good Christian. Neither is one who does not deprive himself of something necessary in order to give it to another who is in need.

7

Those who seek to ease their conscience by attesting: "I'm a serious Catholic, Father, it's really gratifying.... I always go to Mass, every Sunday, I take Communion...." "OK. But how is your relationship with your employees? Do you pay them under the table? Do you pay them a fair wage? Do you make contributions for their pension? For their health and social security?"

Taking the Word to Heart

Isaiah is clear about what God wants from us: feeding the hungry, sheltering the homeless, not turning our backs on those in need. This prophetic challenge is sobering at the beginning of Lent. So often we decide what we're going to give up or do for Lent, and they might be quite worthwhile practices, but we always need to ask ourselves whether we're doing these things for us, for what we imagine God wants, or for the task of spreading the Good News and building up the kingdom of God.

Like the prophets, Pope Francis never hesitates to challenge us to be wary of pious practices that may cover up an unwillingness to help others, especially the poor, the outcast, the refugee, the prisoner. We need to remember that our faith isn't something reserved for Sunday, something that we keep within the walls of the church. Pope Francis's example today and in the beginning of next week make concrete the role of faith in our everyday lives.

Bringing the Word to Life

Take a good look at your Lenten observances today. What are your plans for supper? How often do you look for loopholes in the fasting and abstinence regulations? But also take time to remember how generous God has been to you. How can we show that mercy to others? What will you do today?

Pope Francis Prays

Lord, accompany our Lenten journey
in order that our external observance
may correspond to a profound renewal of the Spirit.

SATURDAY AFTER ASH WEDNESDAY
We're All Sinners
ISAIAH 58:9B–14; LUKE 5:27–32

A WORD FROM POPE FRANCIS

In Buenos Aires there was a well-known confessor. A long line was always awaiting him in the Church of the Most Blessed Sacrament. When he died, I went down into the crypt and the coffin was there; only two old ladies were praying there, but not a single flower. I thought: but this man, who forgave the sins of all the clergy of Buenos Aires, including mine, not even a flower...I went up and went to a florist—because in Buenos Aires there are flower shops at the crossroads, on the streets, where there are people—and I bought flowers, roses.... And I returned and began to decorate the coffin with flowers.... And I looked at the Rosary in his hands.... And immediately it came to mind—the thief that we all have inside of us, don't we?—And while I was arranging the flowers I took the cross off the Rosary, and with a little effort I detached it. At that moment I looked at him and said: "Give me half of your mercy." I felt something powerful that gave me the courage to do this and to say this prayer! And then I put the cross here, in my pocket. But the Pope's shirts don't have pockets, but I always carry it here in a little cloth bag, and that cross has been with me from that moment until today. And when a uncharitable thought against someone comes to mind, my hand always touches it here, always. And I feel the grace!

TAKING THE WORD TO HEART

Pope Francis often tells us that he is no less a sinner than the rest of us. This isn't pious sentiment. He offers examples of his own sins. When he told this story about taking the cross from the rosary of a deceased priest, the media predictably picked up on the stealing angle. But a closer reading of the story shows a much more complex side to the story. He kept the cross with him not (only) as a reminder of his transgression but as a talisman of the revered confessor's own ministry of mercy.

We run from admitting that we're not perfect. Lent calls us back to seeing that God loves us as we are and wants to heal us. We are a mix of light and dark. We do the right things for the wrong reasons and sometimes do the wrong things with the best of intentions. Even something objectively wrong can become, through God's grace, a sign of something holy and healing, a marker along our path that leads us home to God.

Bringing the Word to Life

Think back on some of the events in your life that you may have regretted at the time. Ask God to show you the lessons learned, the ways you grew through those experiences. Regret and shame often cloud our vision and we miss the full impact of our actions. Lent is a time to begin to see clearly, to see our lives as God sees them.

Pope Francis Prays

Lent is a favorable time to intensify spiritual life:
may the practice of fasting be of help to you,
in order to acquire greater mastery of yourselves;
may prayer be the means to entrust your lives to God
and to feel him always nearby;
may the works of mercy help you to live
open to the needs of brothers and sisters.

SUNDAY OF THE FIRST WEEK OF LENT
Wrestling with Temptation
YEAR A: GENESIS 2:7–9, 3:1–7; PSALM 51:3–4, 5–6, 12–13, 17;
ROMANS 5:12–19; MATTHEW 4:1–11
YEAR B: GENESIS 9:8–15; PSALM 25:4–5, 6–7, 8–9;
1 PETER 3:18–22; MARK 1:12–15
YEAR C: DEUTERONOMY 26:4–10; PSALM 91:1–2, 10–11, 12–13, 14–15;
ROMANS 10:8–13; LUKE 4:1–13

A WORD FROM POPE FRANCIS

The tempter seeks to divert Jesus from the Father's plan, that is, from the way of sacrifice, of the love that offers itself in expiation, to make him take an easier path, one of success and power. The duel between Jesus and Satan takes place through strong quotations from Sacred Scripture. The devil, in fact, to divert Jesus from the way of the cross, sets before him false messianic hopes: economic well-being, indicated by the ability to turn stones into bread; a dramatic and miraculous style, with the idea of throwing himself down from the highest point of the Temple in Jerusalem and being saved by angels; and lastly, a shortcut to power and dominion, in exchange for an act of adoration to Satan. These are the three groups of temptations: and we, too, know them well!

Jesus decisively rejects all these temptations and reiterates his firm resolve to follow the path set by the Father, without any kind of compromise with sin or worldly logic. Note well how Jesus responds. He does not dialogue with Satan, as Eve had done in the earthly paradise. Jesus is well aware that there can be no dialogue with Satan, for he is cunning. That is why Jesus chooses to take refuge in the Word of God and responds with the power of this Word. Let us remember this: at the moment of temptation, of our temptations, there is no arguing with Satan, our defense must always be the Word of God! And this will save us.

Taking the Word to Heart

Our temptations aren't likely to come to us from a mysterious figure in a deserted place. But often they revolve around the same basic human drives: hunger, emotional security, personal safety, status, ambition. Sometimes they sneak in through our very desire to help others. We rush in to fix things (or people) that aren't our responsibility. We think sometimes that we know better than anyone—even God—what the answer to a problem or a prayer should be. Pope Francis encourages us to recall during this Lenten season that our salvation lies in God alone. We can take comfort in the fact that Jesus himself was tempted by these things. Seeing his battle with his adversary in more human and less cosmic terms can help us when we're struggling with temptation.

Bringing the Word to Life

By the first Sunday of Lent, our journey into the season is past its first steps, whether they were tentative tiptoes or enthusiastic strides. Take some time today to reflect on the Gospel reading with its three temptations. Decide which one you need to focus on most this year. What will you do to begin to challenge its hold on your life?

Pope Francis Prays

Dear brothers and sisters,
Let us renew the promises of our Baptism:
let us renounce Satan and all his works and seductions
—for he is a seducer—
in order to follow the path of God
and arrive at Easter in the joy of the Spirit.

MONDAY OF THE FIRST WEEK OF LENT
The Least of These
LEVITICUS 19:1–2, 11–18; MATTHEW 25:31–46

A WORD FROM POPE FRANCIS

*H*ow is your health, you who are a good Christian?"—
"Good, thank God; but also, when I need to, I immediately go to
the hospital and, since I belong to the public health system, they
see me right away and give me the necessary medicines."—"It's a
good thing, thank the Lord. But tell me, have you thought about
those who don't have this relationship with the hospital and when
they arrive, they have to wait six, seven, eight hours?"

I think of all the people who live this way here in Rome: children and the elderly who do not have the possibility to be seen by
a doctor. And Lent is the season to think about them and how we
can help these people: "But Father, there are hospitals."—"Yes,
but you have to wait eight hours and then they have you return a
week later." Instead we should be concerned about people in difficulty and ask ourselves: "What are you doing for those people?"

TAKING THE WORD TO HEART

Pope Francis continues his reflection on the central passage from
Isaiah 58. It fits in well with the parable of the Last Judgment from

Matthew's Gospel. Even allowing for the differences between the Italian health care system and our own, we can recognize all too easily our tendency to settle for having our own needs met without thinking about the needs of those who lack our access to the best in health care and medicine, whether in developing countries or in our own cities and rural areas.

Anytime we thank God (or our employers) for our health coverage, we should also give thought to those who don't have these basic needs met in any substantial way. At the very least, we can resist the temptation to criticize the poor for what we might perceive as some "entitlement" because they qualify for Medicaid. But we can do better than that by working through the complex and often vexing issue of reforming our own health care system. While no government program is going to be without its flaws, we have an obligation as Christians to make sure we don't settle for having merely our own needs met.

Bringing the Word to Life

In the parable of the sheep and the goats, Jesus outlines for us the actions that have come to be known as the corporal and spiritual works of mercy. These have been part of our tradition for centuries, but they seem to move in and out of individual and collective conscience. Find a list of these works of mercy and decide on several concrete ways you can live them this Lent.

Pope Francis Prays

Send your Spirit and consecrate every one of us with its anointing,

so that your Church, with renewed enthusiasm, may bring good news to the poor,

proclaim liberty to captives and the oppressed,

and restore sight to the blind.

TUESDAY OF THE FIRST WEEK OF LENT
God Forgives the Maximum
ISAIAH 55:10–11; MATTHEW 6:7–15

A WORD FROM POPE FRANCIS

*I*n the Our Father we say: "Forgive us our debts as we forgive our debtors." This is an equation. If you are not capable of forgiveness, how can God forgive you? The Lord wants to forgive you, but he cannot if you keep your heart closed and mercy cannot enter. One might object: "Father, I forgive, but I cannot forget that awful thing that he did to me…." The answer is to ask the Lord to help you forget. It may be true that one can forgive, but one does not always manage to forget, but an attitude of "You're forgiven, but you'll pay for this" is surely unacceptable. Instead, one must forgive as God forgives, and God forgives the maximum.

TAKING THE WORD TO HEART

No matter how many times we hear reflections such as this on the Our Father, they always seem to startle us. We get familiar with this prayer. It's one of the earliest prayers we learn, one that we say repeatedly in the rosary, at Mass, at many Christian gatherings. And yet our minds allow us to hide behind the familiar words and lose sight of what we're committing ourselves to. While God's mercy has no limits, and he is always ready to forgive, we limit the effects of that forgiveness in our lives when we fail to forgive others. It was true in Jesus's day and it's true in our own day. We forget that we have been forgiven for serious faults and failures and we let ourselves be consumed by petty grudges against people who have slighted us in some way.

Pope Francis reminds us that prayer is the best way to overcome these blind spots in our attitudes toward others. He doesn't say it will be easy. But neither does he let us off the hook. We might smile nervously at his example of payback. But if we search our hearts, we know that we've all been guilty of that desire to hold someone accountable long after we think we've forgiven them.

Bringing the Word to Life

If we don't take time to reflect on the ways we have been forgiven, it will be hard to be merciful to others. And yet we set this as our goal each time we pray the Our Father: "Forgive us our sins as we forgive those who sin against us." Name one person (or several) who come to mind as someone you find difficult to forgive. Hold that person in your mind and heart and slowly pray an Our Father for the intention of forgiveness. Do this as many times as you need to, recalling Jesus's words to Peter: "Not seven but seventy times seven."

POPE FRANCIS PRAYS

We are called as Christians
to proclaim the liberating news
that forgiveness for sins committed is possible,
that God is greater than our sinfulness,
that he freely loves us at all times,
that we were made for communion and eternal life.

WEDNESDAY OF THE FIRST WEEK OF LENT
What Will Your Lent Be Like?
JONAH 3:1–10; LUKE 11:29–32

A WORD FROM POPE FRANCIS

What will your Lent be like?"—"Thank God I have a family who follows the Commandments, we don't have problems...." —"But during Lent is there room in your heart for those who haven't fulfilled the Commandments? Who have made mistakes and are in prison?"—"Not with those people, no...."—"But if you are not in prison it is because the Lord has helped you not to fall. Is there room in your heart for inmates? Do you pray for them, that the Lord may help them change their life?"

TAKING THE WORD TO HEART

The Scripture readings during the first days of Lent take on the religious establishments at the time of Jesus and the days of the Hebrew prophets. They serve also as a warning for those of us today who are immersed in the life of the Church. Whether we're involved in professional or volunteer ministry, daily Mass-goers, or simply people working to improve our spiritual lives, the readings remind us that there's a whole world outside the church doors that needs our gifts as well. Pope Francis takes up this theme with great relish, in part because his daily homilies at the St. Martha Guest House chapel are often given to an audience of priests and professional church workers.

Today's reflection is part of a longer meditation on the response of "good" Catholics to the words of Isaiah 58 that we hear on the Friday after Ash Wednesday. He reminds us of the old adage, "There but for the grace of God go I." It's a reminder that we probably need to reflect on frequently, because the tendency is to fall into thinking, "My own heroic efforts have kept me from falling."

Our first reading from the book of Jonah shows us the dangers good religious people can fall victim to when they think they know better than God who is worthy and who isn't.

Bringing the Word to Life

Jonah seems to relish the thought of the destruction of Nineveh. And yet, the people of Nineveh surprised him when they did, in fact, repent. God surprised him even more when he had mercy on the people. When have you been surprised by an act of genuine repentance? How did you need to change your preconceived ideas as a result?

Pope Francis Prays

You willed that your ministers
would also be clothed in weakness
in order that they may feel compassion
for those in ignorance and error:
let everyone who approaches them feel sought after, loved,
and forgiven by God.

THURSDAY OF THE FIRST WEEK OF LENT
Becoming Merciful
ESTHER C:12, 14–16, 23–25; MATTHEW 7:7–12

A WORD FROM POPE FRANCIS

*G*od's mercy transforms human hearts; it enables us, through the experience of a faithful love, to become merciful in turn. In an ever new miracle, divine mercy shines forth in our lives, inspiring each of us to love our neighbor and to devote ourselves to what the Church's tradition calls the spiritual and corporal works of mercy. These works remind us that faith finds expression in concrete everyday actions meant to help our neighbors in body and spirit. On such things will we be judged.

In the corporal works of mercy we touch the flesh of Christ in our brothers and sisters who need to be fed, clothed, sheltered, visited; in the spiritual works of mercy—counsel, instruction, forgiveness, admonishment, and prayer—we touch more directly our own sinfulness. The corporal and spiritual works of mercy must never be separated. By touching the flesh of the crucified Jesus in the suffering, sinners can receive the gift of realizing that they too are poor and in need. This love alone is the answer to that yearning for infinite happiness and love that we think we can satisfy with the idols of knowledge, power and riches. Yet the danger always remains that by a constant refusal to open the doors of their hearts to Christ who knocks on them in the poor, the proud, rich and powerful will end up condemning themselves and plunging into the eternal abyss of solitude which is hell.

TAKING THE WORD TO HEART

Jesus challenges us to examine our beliefs about the Father. Again and again Jesus shows that God is merciful, loving, waiting to give us everything that is good. We read a passage like this one from Matthew's Gospel and we can't believe that it's that easy; "Ask, and it will be given to you; search, and you will find; knock, and the door will be opened for you. For everyone who asks receives, and everyone who searches finds, and for everyone who knocks, the door will be opened." We might immediately think of unanswered prayers or doors shut against us.

Why might we cling to a belief that God only wants to punish us? It could have something to do with our feelings of personal worthiness. It could also be rooted in our previous experiences of being treated poorly by others. We often form our earliest images of God based on what we know of our parents and other authority figures in our life. But the revelation of the Gospels is that our God is bigger and greater and more loving and trustworthy than any human being we have known.

BRINGING THE WORD TO LIFE

Go out of your way to do something kind for another today, especially if it's something someone asks you to do. Reflect for a moment afterward whether you normally hesitate to respond to similar requests or whether you do them willingly and wholeheartedly. Say a prayer of intercession or thanksgiving as appropriate and resolve to go forward in the spirit of Jesus.

POPE FRANCIS PRAYS

Let us not waste this season of Lent,
so favorable a time for conversion!
We ask this through the maternal intercession
of the Virgin Mary, who, encountering
the greatness of God's mercy
freely bestowed upon her,
was the first to acknowledge her lowliness
and to call herself the Lord's humble servant.

FRIDAY OF THE FIRST WEEK OF LENT
The Holiness of Negotiation
EZEKIEL 18:21–28; MATTHEW 5:20–26

A WORD FROM POPE FRANCIS

*J*esus knows us so well and he knows how we are made because he is the creator, he knows our nature. This is what he suggests: "If you have a problem with a brother—he uses the word adversary—bring yourselves to an agreement." In this way the Lord teaches us a healthy realism: Many times you cannot achieve perfection, but at least you do what you can, you reach an agreement so as not to end up in court. This is the healthy realism of the Catholic Church: the Catholic Church never teaches "either this or this." Rather, the Church says: "this and this." In short, strive for perfection: reconcile yourself with your brother, do not insult him, love him, but should you have any problem at least put yourself in agreement, so as to avoid war.

Jesus always knows how to walk with us, he gives us the ideal, he accompanies us towards the ideal, he frees us from being locked into the rigidity of the law and he tells us: "Do this to the extent that you can." And he understands us well. This is our Lord, it is he who teaches us, saying: "Please, do not insult each other, do not be hypocrites. You go to praise God with the same language with which you insulted your brother. No, do not do that, but do what you can, at least avoid war amongst yourselves, agree with each other."

Allow me to share a term with you which might seem a bit strange, it is the little holiness of negotiation: I cannot do everything, but I want to do everything, I am going to agree with you, at least let us not insult one another, let us not make war and let us live together in peace.

Taking the Word to Heart

When we hear challenging passages from Scripture, we might be tempted to say, "What Jesus really meant to say…" and then we change the message to something that sounds more like what we think God wants us to do. For people who pride themselves on sticking tightly to the rules of the Church, messages of God's mercy and tolerance often seem disorienting. We want to be right more than we want to be reconciled. We want to believe that we're saved and others are damned. We like our world black and white.

For Pope Francis, reflecting on the words and following in the way of Jesus, reconciliation is the better choice, even if it means bending our self-righteousness a bit. There's an old saying, "You can catch more flies with honey than with vinegar." If we focus on finding common ground with one another, we're less likely to end up in irreconcilable disputes. We might never come around to another's point of view completely, but both sides may move closer to the middle through what the pope calls "the little holiness of negotiation."

Bringing the Word to Life

Sometimes going to church and doing "holy things" is easier than the hard work of being reconciled to people in our families, people at work, people who rub us the wrong way. You know what you need to do. How are you going to do it?

Pope Francis Prays

Let us ask the Lord to teach us,
to leave all rigidity, but to go upwards,
to be able to adore and praise God;
that He may teach us to be reconciled with one another;
and also, that He may teach us
to agree with each other to the extent that we can.

SATURDAY OF THE FIRST WEEK OF LENT
Doing the Unthinkable
DEUTERONOMY 26:16–19; MATTHEW 5:43–48

A WORD FROM POPE FRANCIS

*T*here is a healing process for the heart wounded by original sin. It is a journey proposed to everyone, because we all have a heart wounded by sin, everyone. On this path there is no place for hatred. The bar is raised even higher: first, Jesus leads us to give more to our brothers and our friends, and now even to our enemies. In fact, the last step of the stairs to recovery brings with it this recommendation: "Pray for those who persecute you." This commandment—to pray for our enemies—can floor us, because due to the wound that we all have in our hearts, we naturally wish something a bit bad toward an enemy who slanders us, for example. Instead, Jesus tells us: "No, no! Pray for him and do penance for him."

As a boy I heard someone speak about one of the great dictators of the world after the war, and this person said: "May God take him to hell as soon as possible." Though the heart may give this feeling immediately, the new commandment instead says: "Pray for him." Of course, it is easier to pray for someone who is far, far away, for a dictator who is far away, than to pray for those who have hurt me. Yet this is precisely what Jesus asks of us. One might ask: "Why so much generosity, Lord?" Jesus gives the answer precisely in the Gospel: So as to be children of your Father who is in heaven. This healing of the heart leads us to become children. And what does the Father do? "He makes his sun rise on the bad and on the good; he sends rain on the just and on the unjust" because he is the Father of all.

Taking the Word to Heart

"Love your enemies, pray for those who persecute you." We don't want to hear these words of Jesus. Present-day examples of people not only hearing these words but living them draw scorn and derision, often from other Christians. Love and forgiveness can change the world. When we read stories of true forgiveness in terrible circumstances, the people seem heroic, superhuman. But we are all called to do this. Perhaps it's only through God's grace that we can begin. But our faith assures us that we have that grace. The actions of those who perpetrate evil are indeed horrific. Forgiveness doesn't change that fact or mask it somehow. But we forgive because that is our calling, our very nature, as Christians.

Bringing the Word to Life

Pope Francis suggests that we pray for our enemies using their full names. Giving someone a name is a step toward recognizing their humanity, recognizing their relationship to us. It becomes more difficult to keep them in a box and denigrate them with a stereotype. It also makes us more human. We are all children of God.

Pope Francis Prays

May the Lord give us the grace
to pray for our enemies;
to pray for those who wish us ill,
who do not love us;
to pray for those who do us harm,
who persecute us.
We will see that this prayer will bear two fruits:
it will improve our enemy, because prayer is powerful;
and it will make us more as children of the Father.

SUNDAY OF THE SECOND WEEK OF LENT
Do We Listen to Jesus?

YEAR A: GENESIS 12:1–4A; PSALM 33:4–5, 18–19, 20, 22;
2 TIMOTHY 1:8–10; MATTHEW 17:1–9
YEAR B: GENESIS 22:1–2, 9A, 10–13, 15–18; PSALM 116:10, 15, 16–17,
18–19; ROMANS 8:31B–34; MARK 9:2–10
YEAR C: GENESIS 15:5–12, 17–18; PSALM 27:1, 7–8A, 8B–9, 13–14;
PHILIPPIANS 3:17 — 4:1; LUKE 9:28B–36

A WORD FROM POPE FRANCIS

When the Lord is transfigured before Peter, James and John, they hear the voice of God the Father say: "This is my beloved Son! listen to him!" Listen to Jesus! "But, Father, I do listen to Jesus, I listen a lot!" "Yes? What do you listen to?" "I listen to the radio, I listen to the television, I listen to people gossip." We listen to so many things throughout the day, so many things…. But I ask you a question: do we take a little time each day to listen to Jesus, to listen to Jesus's word?

To listen to Jesus, we must be close to him, to follow him, like the crowd in the Gospel who chased him through the streets of Palestine. Jesus did not have a teaching post or a fixed pulpit, he was an itinerant teacher, who proposed his teachings, teachings given to him by the Father, along the streets, covering distances that were not always predictable or easy.

When we hear the Word of Jesus, when we listen to the Word of Jesus and carry it in our heart, this Word grows. Do you know how it grows? By giving it to the other!

TAKING THE WORD TO HEART

Scripture scholars point to the figures of Moses and Elijah as representing the Law (Torah) and the prophets. In this scene from the Transfiguration, we see the combined wisdom of the Hebrew Scriptures and the Christian New Testament. It's not surprising, then, that Pope Francis uses this second Sunday of Lent to impress upon us one of his favorite themes: get to know the Gospels, the Bible, the Word of God, because in doing so, you grow closer to Jesus. Unlike the privileged few who walked and talked with Jesus of Nazareth two thousand years ago, we encounter God most of the time mediated through the inspired words of Scripture. But God's command to Peter, James, and John is the same for us: "Listen to him."

One reason Pope Francis's homilies are so popular is that he has such a realistic grasp of ordinary human nature. He knows what people say and also what they don't say. His decades of pastoral experience, moving familiarly among his flock, have taught him that people are quick to say what they think "Father" wants to hear and not what they actually do, think, or feel. How much we ourselves do this is going to vary from person to person and situation to situation. But we've all known times when we've gotten beneath the surface words to those words that really matter, those words that make a difference, the words that change our lives. This is the Word that God speaks to us if we take time to truly listen.

BRINGING THE WORD TO LIFE

Moments of transfiguration are rare, but when we experience them, they change everything we know about reality. Don't be distracted by the details of what Jesus experienced. Your own may surprise you by its seeming ordinariness. When has this happened for you? How is your life different because of it?

POPE FRANCIS PRAYS

Follow Jesus in order to listen to him.
But also let us listen to Jesus
in his written Word, in the Gospel.
This is what Christian life is.
It is a mission for the whole Church,
for all the baptized, for us all:
listen to Jesus and offer him to others.

MONDAY OF THE SECOND WEEK OF LENT
Who Am I to Judge?
DANIEL 9:4B–10; LUKE 6:36–38

W A WORD FROM POPE FRANCIS

e are all masters, we are all experts, when it comes to justifying ourselves. We all have an alibi to justify our shortcomings, our sins. We so often respond with an 'I don't know!' face, or with an 'I didn't do it, it must have been someone else!' face. We are always ready to play innocent. Before and after confession, in your life, in your prayer, are you able to blame yourself? Or is it easier to blame others?

When one learns to blame himself he is merciful with others. And he is able to say: "Who am I to judge him, if I am capable of doing worse things?" This is an important phrase: "Who am I to judge another?" This is understood in the light of Jesus's words: "Be merciful, just as your Father is merciful," and with his call not to judge. How we like to judge others, to speak ill of them! Yet the Lord is clear: "Stop judging and you will not be judged. Stop condemning and you will not be condemned. Forgive and you will be forgiven." It is certainly not an easy road, which begins with blaming oneself, it begins from that shame before God and from asking forgiveness from Him: ask forgiveness. Precisely from that first step we arrive at what the Lord asks us: to be merciful, to judge no one, to condemn no one, to be generous with others.

Taking the Word to Heart

One of the phrases most likely to be associated with Pope Francis is the one he uses here: "Who am I to judge?" He used it in a conversation with journalists early in his papacy, when someone asked him about gay priests. And he used it again in the summer of 2016 in response to the tragic mass shooting at a gay nightclub in Orlando. Some people have tried to explain it away, saying that he was caught off guard, didn't mean what he said, or perhaps it was a problem of translation. But here we see that it's a phrase that he has thought about deeply and taken to heart. This isn't a question of moral relativism. Rather, it's an openness to the mercy of God not only for oneself but for everyone. If God doesn't judge us for our many failings, who are we to judge others harshly?

Blaming others, especially for something we've done, is an attitude that we ought to outgrow sometime in our toddler years. But like many of the other remnants of original sin (remember Adam and Eve in the garden of Eden), we cling to this finger-pointing, especially when we feel challenged, threatened, or perhaps just embarrassed at being caught in a compromising situation. Pope Francis has been an extraordinary role model in the art of being perfectly human and perfectly Christian. He makes it look and sound so easy, perhaps because he comes to us with the wisdom of decades learning to do this himself.

BRINGING THE WORD TO LIFE

Jesus reserved his harshest words in the Gospels for those who thought they were religiously and spiritually superior to others. As soon as we think we're better than someone else, we set ourselves up for a fall. When are you likely to do this? What might be a better response?

POPE FRANCIS PRAYS

Lord, in this Lenten season,
give us the grace to learn to blame ourselves,
each in his solitude, asking,
Have compassion for me, Lord,
help me to feel shame and give me mercy,
so that I may be merciful with others.

TUESDAY OF THE SECOND WEEK OF LENT
God Is Practical
ISAIAH 1:10, 16–20; MATTHEW 23:1–12

A WORD FROM POPE FRANCIS

How often we find people—ourselves included—so often in the Church who proclaim: "I am a real Catholic!" They should be asked, "What do you do?" How many parents say they are Catholic, but never take the time to speak to their children, to play with their children, to listen to their children? Perhaps they have their parents in a rest home, but they are always busy and cannot go to visit them, leaving them abandoned there. Yet they repeat: "I am a real Catholic. I belong to that association...."

The Lord's mercy is in doing. Being Christian means acting: doing the will of God. And on the last day—because we will all have one—what will the Lord ask us? Will he ask us: "What have you said about me?" No! He will ask about the things we have done. He will ask us about practical things: "I was hungry and you gave me food; I was thirsty and you gave me drink; I was sick and you visited me; I was in prison and you came to me." Because this is Christian life. On the other hand, talk by itself leads us to vanity, to the pretense of being Christian. No, one is not Christian like this!

Taking the Word to Heart

The season of Lent pushes us to go beneath the surface practices and pieties that sometimes characterize our religious life. I often say that the Lent I need always finds me somehow, and it's usually right about the second week. Whatever challenges or activities I've set for myself before Ash Wednesday fall to the wayside, and the big thing that I need to work on meets me head on in the road. It's usually hard to miss, even painfully obvious once I get to that point. It's the sort of thing someone once referred to as "God's clue-by-four" hitting me over the head until I begin to see what's wrong in my life.

The Gospels make this clear over and over again. Talking a good line, saying all the right prayers, doing all the right novenas and devotions aren't going to get us anywhere if our actions aren't in line with the straightforward commands of Jesus: Love one another; feed one another; clothe the naked; shelter the homeless.

Bringing the Word to Life

Have you made a list yet of the corporal and spiritual works of mercy? Today would be a good day to take it out and read through it again. How are you doing on finding creative and concrete ways to carry out these works? We don't need to go to extraordinary lengths. It's more important to make them a regular part of our daily routines. The pope has some suggestions here. What might you add from your own experience?

POPE FRANCIS PRAYS

Lord grant us this wisdom
to properly understand the difference
between talk and action.
Teach us the path of doing
and help us to take that path.

WEDNESDAY OF THE SECOND WEEK OF LENT
A Life of Service
JEREMIAH 18:18–20; MATTHEW 20:17–28

A WORD FROM POPE FRANCIS

*J*esus speaks a language of humiliation, of death, of redemption, and they speak a language of climbers: who will climb the highest in terms of power? They were tempted by a worldly way of thinking but they were not the only ones. The mother of James and John too, went to Jesus to ask that one of her sons be on the right and the other on the left, when He arrived in the Kingdom. As if she were to ask today that one be prime minister and the other the minister of the economy, so as to share all the power. It is worldly thinking to ask who is the greatest. Jesus takes care to tell them: "If any one would be first, he must be last of all and servant of all."

On the path that Jesus points out to us in order to go forward, service is the rule. The one who is greatest is the one who serves most, who is most at the service of others, not the one who boasts, who seeks power, money, vanity, pride.

Taking the Word to Heart

Jesus knows what lies ahead for him and it's not pleasant. His followers seem too absorbed in their own ambitions to hear what he's saying. We've been on both ends of situations like this. We've been the one who desperately needs to be heard, understood, encouraged, consoled. And we've been the ones too preoccupied to be aware of the needs of those around us. Even when we think we're not putting all our energy into getting ahead—at work, in school, among the neighbors—we will find subtle indications that we're overly concerned about our reputation and image. Sometimes we're striving (or struggling) to meet the expectations others have of us. Other times we're putting unrealistic expectations on our children, our employees, our friends. The scene in today's Gospel reminds us that the temptation to seek power and status worms its way into our lives from a variety of sources.

Bringing the Word to Life

Take time today to listen carefully to your family and friends. Stop yourself from the temptation to give advice or turn the conversation to your own needs. Notice what a difference it makes to simply be present to what another person is saying.

POPE FRANCIS PRAYS

Let us ask the Virgin Mary—
who was humble all her life—
to lead us every day on the way of humility

…

seeking nothing in return,
so that we might become worthy
of the divine reward.

THURSDAY OF THE SECOND WEEK OF LENT
Seeing the Invisible Ones
JEREMIAH 17:5–10; LUKE 16:19–31

A WORD FROM POPE FRANCIS

*D*idn't God who is Father have mercy on this man? Didn't he knock at his heart in order to move him? Yes, he was at the door, he was at the door, in the person of Lazarus. Lazarus—this man has a name. Lazarus, with his needs and his miseries, his disease, was actually the Lord who was knocking at the door, so that this man would open his heart and mercy could enter. Instead, the rich man didn't see, because he was closed, and for him there was nothing beyond the door.

The Gospel passage is helpful to all of us at the midpoint of the Lenten journey, in order to raise a few questions: Am I on the path of life or on the path of lies? How many locks do I still have on my heart? Where is my joy: in doing or talking? Is my joy in going outside of myself in order to meet others, in order to help, or is my joy in having everything organized, locked up inside myself?

TAKING THE WORD TO HEART

Pope Francis's words today remind me of when I was first living on my own in a new city, working at a new job, struggling a bit in my introverted way to make friends and find my way. A dear friend would listen to me whine for just so long and then would say, "What are you doing to get outside of yourself?" It's a good question to ask ourselves and one another. As the pope says, it's a good question for this midpoint in the season of Lent.

The story of Lazarus and the rich man hits home for many of us. We like to be comfortable and secure behind our locked doors, in our gated suburban communities. We don't want to make eye contact with the homeless people under our freeway bridges or the people holding cardboard signs asking for help. We feel guilty when those signs say "God bless" because we know that God wants us to help these people. But instead of letting that guilt move us to do good, we make excuses and blame the people begging for their own condition.

Pope Francis has done so much to show us concrete ways to minister to the poor and the homeless. He has been the motivation behind showers for the homeless in St. Peter's Square, hosting gatherings of homeless people in the Sistine Chapel (because beauty is sometimes as much of a need as bread), and many other gestures that go far beyond the merely symbolic. When he admonishes us, we know that he has gone before us on the Gospel road.

Bringing the Word to Life

How often do we, like the rich man in today's Gospel, consistently ignore the beggars at our gates? At the very least, take time to see them. Smile. Make eye contact. Set aside some amount of cash each week to give to people you see on the street. If you don't want to give money, keep snacks or personal care items in your car. Don't just feel guilty today; take action!

Pope Francis Prays

Let us ask the Lord for the grace
to always see the Lazarus who knocks at our heart
and for the grace to go outside of ourselves
with generosity, with an attitude of mercy,
so that God's mercy can enter our heart.

FRIDAY OF THE SECOND WEEK OF LENT
Wanting What Others Have
GENESIS 37:3–4, 12–13A, 17B–28A; MATTHEW 21:33–43, 45–46

A WORD FROM POPE FRANCIS

*T*he Lord has lent us life, and with it, the promise that he would come to save us. Yet this people saw a profitable business venture in it: "The vineyard is beautiful, let's take it, it's ours!" Disobeying the word of God is like trying to say: "This is no longer God's Word: now it is ours." As the word of God died in the heart of these people, it can also die in our hearts. And yet the word does not end there, for it is alive in the heart of the simple, the humble, the people of God. The simple crowd followed Jesus because what Jesus said did them great good and warmed their hearts. They didn't use the Word of God for their own interests. Rather, they listened and sought to be better.

What can we do so as not to kill the Word of God, so as not to make ourselves masters of this word, to be docile, and not to lock up the Holy Spirit? Two simple ways: humility and prayer.

TAKING THE WORD TO HEART

In both readings today, jealousy and envy are at the root of violent acts. Genesis would tell us that they were at the root of the first murder. This happens in varying degrees all around us. It's not limited to any one economic class or social status. Sometimes people with very few possessions are quick to share what little they have with others. And sometimes people who have more than they can possibly use will not only hoard that, but seek to acquire more. We don't always know what motivates people to envy. Sometimes it's just what my father would have called "cussed human nature." It might be a shred of original sin. At the same time, it might be divine grace that moves us to generosity.

We don't need to waste a lot of time asking why or how. Rather, we need to recognize these negative traits for what they are— sin—and pray for God to show us how to uproot them from our lives. Gratitude for what we have and mercy toward others will go a long way to keeping us right in God's eyes.

BRINGING THE WORD TO LIFE

It's easy to deny that we're envious or jealous. But what does the word *humility* suggest to you? Do you find yourself thinking of it as a positive or negative trait? In what way can you listen to the Word of God and seek to be a better person?

POPE FRANCIS PRAYS

Lord grant us the grace of humility
to look upon Jesus as the Savior
who speaks to us: he speaks to me!
Open our hearts to the Holy Spirit,
who gives power to these words.
May we receive this word and obey it.

SATURDAY OF THE SECOND WEEK OF LENT
Giving It All Away
MICAH 7:14–15, 18–20; LUKE 15:1–3, 11–32

A WORD FROM POPE FRANCIS

*E*ach one of us is that son who has squandered his freedom on false idols, illusions of happiness, and has lost everything. But God does not forget us, the Father never abandons us. He is a patient father, always waiting for us! He respects our freedom, but he remains faithful forever. And when we come back to him, he welcomes us like children into his house, for he never ceases, not for one instant, to wait for us with love. And his heart rejoices over every child who returns. He is celebrating because he is joy. God has this joy, when one of us sinners goes to him and asks his forgiveness.

What is the danger? It is that we presume we are righteous and judge others. We also judge God, because we think that he should punish sinners, condemn them to death, instead of forgiving. So yes, then we risk staying outside the Father's house! Like the older brother in the parable, who rather than being content that his brother has returned, grows angry with the father who welcomes him and celebrates. If in our heart there is no mercy, no joy of forgiveness, we are not in communion with God, even if we observe all of his precepts, for it is love that saves, not the practice of precepts alone. It is love of God and neighbor that brings fulfillment to all the Commandments. And this is the love of God, his joy: forgiveness.

TAKING THE WORD TO HEART

When we realize that the road we have been following, the life we have been leading, may not be the one that is best for us, we must have the humility to admit that we have strayed, that we have been mistaken, that God knows better than we the life that will lead us to him.

Nothing is more difficult than admitting that we have failed, that we have sinned. We feel haunted by the past.

No matter how willing we are to do penance and suffer and take on the heavy burden of our guilt, in the end the greatest humility is accepting the role the Lord has written for us. Like the lavishly forgiving father in the Gospel story, all that the Lord asks is that we come home. We must accept our roles as sons and daughters and not refuse this great gift of love by insisting that we're only hired hands. We are all children of the Father, we have all sinned, but we are all welcome in our Father's house. We must live as a forgiving and as a forgiven people.

Bringing the Word to Life

Most of us can identify with one of the two brothers in this familiar parable. We know what it's like to come to our senses and realize we've taken a wrong turn. Do we also know how to admit that maybe we're not as righteous as we think we are?

Pope Francis Prays

Let's all think of a person
with whom we are annoyed,
with whom we are angry,
someone we do not like.
Let us think of that person and in silence,
at this moment,
let us pray for this person
and let us become merciful with this person.

SUNDAY OF THE THIRD WEEK OF LENT
God's Plans for Us

YEAR A: EXODUS 17:3–7; PSALM 95:1–2, 6–7, 8–9;
ROMANS 5:1–2, 5–8; JOHN 4:5–42
YEAR B: EXODUS 20:1–17; PSALM 19:8, 9, 10, 11;
1 CORINTHIANS 1:22–25; JOHN 2:13–25
YEAR C: EXODUS 3:1–8A, 13–15; PSALM 103:1–2, 3–4, 6–7, 8, 11; 1
CORINTHIANS 10:1–6, 10–12; LUKE 13:1–9

A WORD FROM POPE FRANCIS

*J*esus's thirst was not so much for water, but for the encounter with a parched soul. Jesus needed to encounter the Samaritan woman in order to open her heart: he asks for a drink so as to bring to light her own thirst.

The outcome of that encounter by the well was the woman's transformation. She had gone to draw water from the well, but she found another kind of water, the living water of mercy from which gushes forth eternal life. She found the water she had always sought! She runs to the village, that village which had judged her, condemned her and rejected her, and she announces that she has met the Messiah: the one who has changed her life.

In this Gospel passage we likewise find the impetus to "leave behind our water jar," the symbol of everything that is seemingly important, but loses all its value before the love of God. We all have one, or more than one! I ask you, and myself: "What is your interior water jar, the one that weighs you down, that distances you from God?" Let us set it aside a little and with our hearts; let us hear the voice of Jesus offering us another kind of water, another water that brings us close to the Lord. And so we must tell of the marvelous things the Lord can do in our hearts when we have the courage to set aside our own water jar.

Taking the Word to Heart

The Samaritan woman has known pain and disappointment and the restless search for a life of happiness and meaning. We too thirst for something real, something that will refresh us. But in our desperation we often settle for far less than we deserve, because the life we know demands less of us than the life we dream.

Jesus challenges the woman to believe once more, to risk one more time, to give new life one more chance. He challenges her to tell her story, to listen to the story he has to tell, to believe that this time it can be different.

The Lord is never surprised by our restlessness, our disappointment, our fearful, hurting challenges. Together Jesus and the woman explore the stories of needs and wounds and beliefs. We are the stories of our past—stories we tell, stories other people tell—but we can become the stories God tells for our future.

The townspeople hear the woman's story, which attracts them to Jesus. They have heard because they left what they were doing and took time to listen. The story Jesus tells is good news to the Samaritans and they celebrate the promise and refreshment it brings to their lives.

Bringing the Word to Life

Lent calls us to step aside from our ordinary routines, to spend time listening to God, to believe that we can tell our stories in a new way. The word of God challenges us to explore the story of our faith once more and discover for ourselves that Jesus really is "the savior of the world." Reflect on your first real encounter with Jesus. What would you say to him if you met him this afternoon? What questions would you ask? What deep thirst needs to be quenched? What water jar do you need to abandon?

Pope Francis Prays

Jesus, give me a drink that will quench my thirst forever.
Jesus, change my life!
Jesus, fill me with joy!
Amen.

MONDAY OF THE THIRD WEEK OF LENT
Seeing Those Closest to Us
2 KINGS 5:1–15A; LUKE 4:24–30

A WORD FROM POPE FRANCIS

*I*n our imagination salvation must come from something great, from something majestic: only the powerful can save us, those who have strength, who have money, who have power, these people can save us. Instead, God's plan is different. Thus, they feel disdain because they cannot understand that salvation comes only from little things, from the simplicity of the things of God. When Jesus proposes the way of salvation, he never speaks of great things, but only little things. The little thing is represented by bathing in the Jordan and by the little village of Nazareth. Disdain is a luxury that only the vain, the proud allow themselves.

TAKING THE WORD TO HEART

Every day people begin extreme diets because they simply can't believe that losing weight is simply a matter of burning more calories than they consume. Exotic dietary supplements and steroids in sports fuel the belief in a magic formula to ensure victory when hard work and training isn't enough. Ads for new pharmaceuticals herald the next cure for whatever disease is holding us back. We overlook the simple, everyday ways to better health and well-being because they don't make any remarkable claims to instant results.

Our technology and communication methods might be twenty-first century, but the impulse to seek a spectacular, magic solution to the common plight of humanity is as old as our Scripture readings today. Naaman seeks healing, but he's also hoping for a great spectacle from the famed man of God. The people in Jesus's hometown are hoping that he will wow them with the wonders they've heard he performed in other towns. But he disappoints their expectations and they fail to see the wonder that he is.

The virtue of humility reminds us that the ordinary and the everyday is often where God's gifts shine most brightly. The quiet person we overlook in a meeting might have the solution to a vexing work issue. The chicken soup your grandma made when you had a cold really does have healing properties. The friend who listens patiently while you work out a difficult time in a relationship isn't giving you advice about a quick fix, but the solution you discover in the process has long-lasting effects.

BRINGING THE WORD TO LIFE

Lent is a fine time to examine our attitudes toward everyone in our lives. Take time to acknowledge some contribution by someone you have previously overlooked or dismissed as insignificant and unworthy of recognition.

POPE FRANCIS PRAYS

Lord, give us the grace
to understand that the only way to salvation
is the folly of the Cross,
the annihilation of the Son of God,
of his becoming small.

TUESDAY OF THE THIRD WEEK OF LENT
Forgive and Forget?
DANIEL 3:25, 34–43; MATTHEW 18:21–35

A WORD FROM POPE FRANCIS

When God forgives, his forgiveness is so great that it is as if he has forgotten. Once we are at peace with God through his mercy, if we ask the Lord: "Do you remember that bad thing that I did?" he might answer: "Which one? I don't remember...." This is completely the opposite of what we do, and which often comes out when we gossip: "This person did this, he did this, he did that...." We do not forget, and we keep an ancient, mediaeval and modern history for many people. The reason for this can be found in the fact that we do not have a merciful heart.

It is not easy to forgive; it is not easy. In many families siblings argue over the inheritance from their parents, and then don't say hello to one another for the rest of their lives; so many couples fight, then hatred grows and grows, and that family ends up destroyed. These people are not capable of forgiveness. This is bad.

Lent prepares our heart to receive God's forgiveness. But to receive it and then do the same with others: heartfelt forgiveness.

To have an attitude that leads us to say: "You might never say hello to me, but in my heart I have forgiven you."

TAKING THE WORD TO HEART

"How often must I forgive?" Peter's question is one that we ask ourselves more times than we might be willing to admit. "How often must I forgive?" Jesus is uncompromising in his response: as many times as necessary. Forgiving others (and sometimes ourselves) might be one of the hardest Gospel commands to follow. It's right up there with loving our enemies, another practice that has forgiveness at its core.

Psychologists will often tell people that they can forgive but not expect to forget. This is probably sound advice from a purely human perspective. Nor does forgiveness deny that an injury happened. It acknowledges the hurt and reaches beyond it. If we're carrying grudges, we're the ones who are going to get tired. This is the point Pope Francis is making here.

I've often heard Peter's question in terms of forgiving someone who does the same bad thing over and over again. But the pope's reflection has me wondering if perhaps we don't also struggle with having to keep forgiving the same offense over again because we keep taking it back.

Bringing the Word to Life

Pope Francis is on target when he uses examples of family members failing to forgive. It's one thing to forgive someone more distant from us. But with our family, we have so much past history that smolders beneath the surface, needing only one careless word or act to fan it into flame. And we have to see one another at family functions. If you need to forgive someone in your family (or ask for forgiveness) find a way to make that happen before Easter this year.

Pope Francis Prays

In forgiving we open our heart
for God's mercy to enter and forgive us.
We all have reasons to ask God's forgiveness:
"Let us forgive, and we shall be forgiven."

WEDNESDAY OF THE THIRD WEEK OF LENT
Navigation for the Christian Journey
DEUTERONOMY 4:1, 5–9; MATTHEW 5:17–19

A WORD FROM POPE FRANCIS

*W*e can imagine the context in which Jesus delivered his sermon on the Beatitudes. Jesus, the crowds and the disciples were on the mountain, and Jesus began to speak and taught the new law, which does not erase the old one, because he himself said that every last iota of the old law must be accomplished. In fact, Jesus perfects the old law, the door to its fullness, and this is the new law, that which we call the Beatitudes. They are indeed the Lord's new law for us, the guide for the journey, the itinerary; they are the navigators of the Christian life: it is precisely here, on this road, according to the indications of this navigator, that we can move forward in our Christian life.

The Beatitudes are the guide for the journey that leads us to the kingdom of God. The Beatitudes are the ticket, the guide sheet for our life, so as to avoid getting lost and losing ourselves.

TAKING THE WORD TO HEART

As Jesus begins the Sermon on the Mount, he makes it clear that he is going beyond the law of Moses but not replacing it. We might think of the commandments as the minimum requirement and the Beatitudes as the more mature, deeper expression of the law God places in our hearts. Pope Francis describes the Beatitudes as an internal navigation system, a GPS for our faith.

If we think about the Ten Commandments, we realize that most of us stay well within their boundaries. But the Beatitudes make it clear that while our actions might not betray us, our thoughts and attitudes often do. The Beatitudes narrow the track, keep us moving in the right direction.

BRINGING THE WORD TO LIFE

Pope Francis often concludes his homilies with an encouragement to read the day's Gospel passage over again. Take his advice and read chapter five of Matthew's Gospel. Select one verse that inspires you and one verse that challenges you. Resolve to act on them in some way during the rest of Lent.

POPE FRANCIS PRAYS

The New Covenant consists exactly in this:
in recognizing oneself, in Christ,
enveloped in God's mercy and compassion.
This is what fills our heart with joy,

and this is what makes our life
a beautiful and credible testimony
of God's love for all the brothers and sisters
we meet everyday.

THURSDAY OF THE THIRD WEEK OF LENT
Closed Hearts
JEREMIAH 7:23–28; LUKE 11:14–23

A WORD FROM POPE FRANCIS

This is the story, the history of failed faithfulness, the history of closed hearts, of hearts that would not let God's mercy enter, which had forgotten the word forgiveness—"Forgive me, Lord!"—simply because they did not feel they were sinners: they felt they were the judges of others. And this history goes on for centuries. Jesus explains this failed faithfulness with two clear words in order to end the discussion with these hypocrites: "Whoever is not with me is against me." Either you are faithful, with your heart open to God who is faithful to you, or you are against him. Someone may think that there is perhaps a middle ground for negotiations, to escape the clarity of Jesus's words. In essence, there is a way out: "Confess, sinner!" Because if you say, "I am a sinner," your heart opens, God's mercy enters, and you begin to be faithful. If you do not feel you are a sinner, you have started off wrong.

Taking the Word to Heart

One of the most common attitudes that separates us from others is defensiveness. From international relations to religious denominations to our own schools, workplaces, and families, we close ourselves off to keep from being hurt. When we've done this for a long time, we begin to believe that we're right and everyone else is wrong. We nurse our grudges and resentments. We become trapped by our anger. No matter how right we might have been in the first place, an unwillingness to let go, to forgive, to move forward, will always rebound to hurt us again. It's difficult to let ourselves be open and vulnerable. We struggle to admit that our way might not be the only way. We don't want to see the world through another's eyes.

We need to cultivate a belief that we're all part of the human family. Whatever divides us can't be more important than what unites us. As soon as we say, "I'm right and you're wrong," we've lost the willingness, perhaps even the ability, to see a situation or issue from both sides. Working at empathy and understanding can help widen our horizons and open us to insights that we may have lacked before.

Bringing the Word to Life

Empathy is invaluable for seeing someone else's side of a controversial issue. But reason, too, has its place. We all have issues that we feel strongly about, judging those on the other side harshly and perhaps unfairly. Choose one such issue and take time to research both sides. Challenge yourself to discover three arguments for the opposite side that would stand up in a debate or a courtroom.

Pope Francis Prays

Let us ask for the grace
that our hearts not harden,
that they be open to God's mercy.
Let us ask for the grace of faithfulness.
Let us ask for the grace to ask forgiveness
when we find we are unfaithful.

FRIDAY OF THE THIRD WEEK OF LENT
The Mystery of Love
HOSEA 14:2–10; MARK 12:28B–34

A WORD FROM POPE FRANCIS

[Christ's passion] is all a great mystery of love and mercy. Our words are poor and insufficient to express it fully. We may find helpful the experience of a young woman, not very well known, who wrote sublime pages about the love of Christ. Her name was Julian of Norwich. She was illiterate, this girl who had visions of the passion of Jesus and who then, after becoming a recluse, described, with simple but deep and intense language, the meaning of merciful love. She said: "Then our good Lord asked me: 'Are you glad that I suffered for you?' I answered him: 'Yes, good Lord, and I am most grateful to you; yes, good Lord, may You be blessed.' Then Jesus, our good Lord, said: 'If you are glad, so too am I. Having suffered the passion for you is for me joy, happiness, eternal bliss; and if I could suffer more I would.'" This is our Jesus, who says to each of us: "If I could suffer more for you, I would." How beautiful these words are! They allow us to truly understand the immense and boundless love that the Lord has for each one of us.

Taking the Word to Heart

Today's Gospel is clear: Love God, love others, love yourself. Jesus tells us this is the greatest commandment. If we do this, keeping the other commandments will fall into place with little effort. Sometimes Lent seems like a series of difficult tasks that we toil over to show our spiritual strength and endurance. Julian of Norwich and the other mystics remind us that it's not about what we do, it's about what God does. Our Lenten practices should make room in our lives to contemplate the great mystery of love. If we lose sight of that, then the fasting and prayers become empty gestures. Our almsgiving contributes money to a good cause but we lose sight of our own place in that good work.

Bringing the Word to Life

Often the best way to understand the love of God is to reflect on what we would be willing to do for someone we love dearly, or what another would do—or has done—for us. Human love is an image of divine love. Spend some time today reflecting on the depth of your closest relationships. Give thanks to the God who dwells in the midst of that love.

POPE FRANCIS PRAYS

Let us allow ourselves
to be wrapped in this mercy
which comes to meet us;
as we keep our gaze fixed on
the passion and death of the Lord,
let us receive in our heart his boundless love
and, in silence, await the Resurrection.

SATURDAY OF THE THIRD WEEK OF LENT
Holy Humility
HOSEA 6:1–6; LUKE 18:9–14

A WORD FROM POPE FRANCIS

I once heard a beautiful saying: "There is no saint without a past nor a sinner without a future." The Church is not a community of perfect people, but of disciples on a journey, who follow the Lord because they know they are sinners and in need of his pardon. Thus, Christian life is a school of humility which opens us to grace.

Such behavior is not understood by those who have the arrogance to believe they are "just" and to believe they are better than others. Hubris and pride do not allow one to recognize him- or herself as in need of salvation, but rather prevent one from seeing the merciful face of God and from acting with mercy. They are a barrier. Hubris and pride are a barrier that prevents a relationship with God. Yet, this is precisely Jesus's mission: coming in search of each of us, in order to heal our wounds and to call us to follow him with love.

TAKING THE WORD TO HEART

We spend a great deal of energy comparing ourselves to others. Whether this makes us feel superior or inferior, what it keeps us from is being the person God has called us to be. For all that we have in common with one another, we also have quirks, foibles, and great gifts that are ours alone, part of what makes us unique individuals. Our past experiences, good and bad, will influence our present and our future. God's grace enables us to learn from our past, to shape our future, but also to live with great gratitude and humility in the present.

One thing becomes clear when we become familiar with the lives of the saints: They keep their focus not on themselves, not on those around them, but on God and on the work that God has called them to do. For them, it's all about the work. Earthly honors and even divine consolations are not the source or reward of their activity. They remain grounded in God's merciful love.

BRINGING THE WORD TO LIFE

If you don't already do so, begin to keep a gratitude journal. At the end of each day, write a list of things for which you are grateful. It may feel forced and artificial at first, but it will begin

to color your days as you become more aware of those moments
that will make it to your list.

POPE FRANCIS PRAYS

Dear brothers and sisters,
all of us are invited to the table of the Lord.
Let us make our own this invitation
and sit beside the Lord together with his disciples.
Let us learn to look with mercy
and to recognize each of them as fellow guests at the table.
We are all disciples who need
to experience and live the comforting word of Jesus.
We all need to be nourished by the mercy of God,
for it is from this source that our salvation flows.

SUNDAY OF THE FOURTH WEEK OF LENT
Learning to See
YEAR A: 1 SAMUEL 16:1B, 6–7, 10–13; PSALM 23:1–3A, 3B–4, 5, 6;
EPHESIANS 5:8–14; JOHN 9:1–41
YEAR B: 2 CHRONICLES 36:14–16, 19–23; PSALM 137:1–2, 3, 4–5, 6;
EPHESIANS 2:4–10; JOHN 3:14–21
YEAR C: JOSHUA 5:9A, 10–12; PSALM 34:2–3, 4–5, 6–7;
2 CORINTHIANS 5:17–21; LUKE 15:1–3, 11–32

A WORD FROM POPE FRANCIS

*O*ur lives are sometimes similar to that of the blind man who opened himself to the light, who opened himself to God, who opened himself to his grace. Sometimes unfortunately they are similar to that of the doctors of the law: from the height of our pride we judge others, and even the Lord! Today, we are invited to open ourselves to the light of Christ in order to bear fruit in our lives, to eliminate unchristian behaviors; we are all Christians but we all, everyone sometimes has unchristian behaviors, behaviors that are sins.

Do I have an open heart or a closed heart? Is it open or closed to God? Open or closed to my neighbor? We are always closed to some degree which comes from original sin, from mistakes, from errors. We need not be afraid! Let us open ourselves to the light of the Lord, he awaits us always in order to enable us to see better, to give us more light, to forgive us.

TAKING THE WORD TO HEART

The man who receives new sight grows in wonder and the promise of new possibilities. He searches for Jesus, wants to know more about this person who healed him. He accepts the healing, perhaps because for so many years he accepted his affliction. The religious authorities reject both the man who has been healed and the one who brought about the healing because such an encounter clashes with their worldview and their rules. The disciples see the man as an example of an interesting theological question. They're interested in the "sin" that may have caused the man's blindness. It may never have occurred to them that the man could be healed. And the man's parents simply want to distance themselves from the whole experience. Instead of rejoicing at their son's new opportunities, they see only the threat from the authorities.

Pope Francis has repeatedly done and said things that have shocked us into seeing people, situations, and even our religious structures in a new light. He opens our eyes to the incredible mercy of God, to the diversity of the human condition, to the possibilities for a future marked by unity and acceptance. He lives his faith in a God of surprises. Our initial response might be one of resistance, of not wanting to see the world in a different way than has been our custom. But faith calls us to open our eyes and truly see.

BRINGING THE WORD TO LIFE

Think about something Pope Francis has said or done during the course of his papacy thus far that surprised or even shocked you. Find out the context or more about what he said. Take some time to look at the issue from a variety of angles, learning to see what God might be asking of you, of the Church, of humanity, through this issue.

POPE FRANCIS PRAYS

May Mary, who is the Mother of Mercy,
place in our hearts
the certitude that we are loved by God.
May she be close to us in moments of difficulty
and give us the sentiments of her Son,
so our Lenten journey may be an experience
of forgiveness, of welcome, and of charity.

MONDAY OF THE FOURTH WEEK OF LENT
God's Dream for Us
ISAIAH 65:17–21; JOHN 4:43–54

A WORD FROM POPE FRANCIS

We are the dream of God who, truly in love, wants to change our life through love. He only asks us to have the faith to let Him do so. We can only cry for joy before a God who re-creates us. God thinks about each one of us, loves us, dreams of us, dreams of the joy that He will rejoice with us. Have you ever thought, "The Lord dreams about me, he thinks about me, I am in the mind, in the heart of the Lord"? Have you ever thought, "The Lord is capable of changing my life"?

The Lord is capable of changing us, through love: He is in love with us. What do I have to do? The answer is simple: "Believe. Believe that the Lord can change me."

Faith is giving space to this love of God; it is making room for the power of God, for the power of One who loves me, who is in love with me and who wants this joy with me. This is faith. This is believing: it is making room for the Lord to come and change me.

Taking the Word to Heart

In today's Gospel, a royal official asks Jesus to heal his son. Jesus's first response is a bit defensive: "Unless you people see signs and wonders you will not believe." But the royal official reminds him that this isn't about religious disputes or even the curiosity and amazement of the crowds. This is a simple human need, born of the love of a father for his son and the desperation of a serious illness. The royal official has only one thought in mind: His son is ill and he believes this man can heal him. His directness reminds Jesus of what's essential: life, healing, love.

Too often we live our lives and our faith as a transaction, an exchange of good deeds for God's reward, of work done for payment, of actions and reactions. Pope Francis reminds us that our faith is rather a love affair, a dream, a joyful, passionate embrace that doesn't stop to ask about worth or merit or judgment. When we are caught up in the ecstasy of love, we lose our tendency to stand outside ourselves and consider each action, each thought. When we can bring this to our faith life, we discover the wonderful things God has in mind for us, for our loved ones, for our future.

Bringing the Word to Life

Do something extravagantly loving for someone close to you today. As you do it, let yourself believe that this is the kind of thing God wants to do for you, is doing for you. Before you fall asleep tonight, think of some change you long to see in your life. Believe that God will dream that change into being for you.

Pope Francis Prays

The Lord can change us,
he wants to change us,
he loves to change us.
And this he does through love.
He only asks us for our faith:
to give space to his love
so it may act and bring about a change of life in us.

TUESDAY OF THE FOURTH WEEK OF LENT
It's Never Too Late
EZEKIEL 47:1–9, 12; JOHN 5:1–3A, 5–16

A WORD FROM POPE FRANCIS

*J*esus is presented with a defeated man who had lost hope. A sick man, not just paralyzed but afflicted with another, much worse disease, sloth. Sloth made him sad, lazy. Another person would have found a way to get there in time. But this man, overcome by thirty-eight years of illness, didn't want to be healed, didn't have the strength. At the same time, he had a bitterness of spirit: "Someone else gets there before me and I am left aside." He also had a little resentment. He was really a sad soul, defeated, defeated by life.

This story happens often in life: a man—a woman—who feels sick in spirit, sad, who has made many mistakes in life, at a certain point feels the water stirring. It is the Holy Spirit who moves something. Or the person hears a word and reacts: "I want to go!" Thus they find courage and go. But how often today in Christian communities does that man find the doors closed. Perhaps he hears: "You cannot, no you cannot; you've made mistakes here and you cannot. If you want to come, come to Mass on Sunday, but stop there, don't do anything more." Thus it happens that what the Holy Spirit does in people's hearts, Christians destroy with the psychology of the doctors of the law.

And if the people are wounded what does Jesus do? Does he rebuke them for being wounded? No, he comes and carries them on his shoulders. This is called mercy. God speaks of this when he rebukes his people: "I desire mercy, not sacrifice."

Who are you, who close the door of your heart to a man, to a woman who wants to improve, to rejoin the People of God, because the Holy Spirit has stirred his or her heart?

Taking the Word to Heart

Often the changes we need to make in our lives seem overwhelming until we realize that taking just that first step is all we need. It's not some sort of magic—the angel stirring the pool—that's missing. Sometimes we hesitate to ask for the help that we need. Instead we blame other people for getting in our way, for not reaching out. We see our weakness in a new light. Sometimes we get into a habit of complaining about all the things that are wrong and we don't take time to see what small thing we can do to improve the situation.

It might be that we thought Lent was going to be the opportunity for us to make these changes this year. We were going to stop eating junk food, quit smoking, give up drinking, exercise more, pray more. But then we ran into one obstacle or another and it became an excuse not to make those changes. It's easier to blame others than to take responsibility for our own actions or inaction.

The pope also challenges us. Pope Francis is here to remind us that if we are made in the image of God, we can find healing, we can respond to the stirrings of the spirit, we can open our hearts to those who, like us, have made mistakes and now seek mercy, forgiveness, and peace.

BRINGING THE WORD TO LIFE

Think back to the commitments you made on Ash Wednesday. Be honest about how well you've kept those commitments. Make a list of the excuses you've made to yourself or others about your failures. Now pick one and recommit to it for the rest of the Lenten season.

POPE FRANCIS PRAYS

Let us ask the Lord today
for conversion to the mercy of Jesus:

only in this way will the law be fulfilled,
because the law is to love God and neighbor, as ourselves.

WEDNESDAY OF THE FOURTH WEEK OF LENT
The Work That Is Ours to Do
ISAIAH 49:8–15; JOHN 5:17–30

A WORD FROM POPE FRANCIS
Pope Francis said he will continue pressing for a church that is open and understanding despite opposition from some clerics who "say no to everything."

"They do their work and I do mine," the pope said when asked, "What is your relationship with ultraconservatives in the church?"

The question was posed by Joaquin Morales Sola, a journalist for the Argentine newspaper *La Nacion*, in an interview published on July 3. The Vatican newspaper, *L'Osservatore Romano,* published a translation of the interview July 5.

"I want a church that is open, understanding, that accompanies families who are hurting," Pope Francis said.

Some church leaders do not agree with his approach, but "I continue my course without looking over my shoulder," he said, adding that he does not try to silence them. "I don't cut off heads. I've never liked doing that."

Taking the Word to Heart

As Jesus responds to those who question his identity as the Son of God, he puts it in terms of the work that God does in the world. From the beginning of creation, it is God's work that keeps all the universe in existence. Jesus shares in that work.

Pope Francis shows us by his deeds and occasionally by his words that his work as pope is to lead God's people in the way of the Gospel. In any religious organization the foibles and weaknesses of human society can become more visible and at times more important than the underlying good work that's being done. It's part of the pope's responsibility—any pope in history—to rise above the controversy and the squabbling to focus on doing God's work in the world.

We know that in our own lives—at home, at work, in school, in various organizations—that the less admirable behaviors can distract from the work at hand. We spend more time complaining about what other people are doing or not doing than we spend doing the work that is ours to do.

Bringing the Word to Life

Reflect today on the work that you do, whatever that might be. Ask yourself how focusing on that work can keep you from falling into the various snares that Pope Francis often talks about—gossip, backbiting, jealousy, despair. How can your work help you to further the way of God in the world? When you feel disillusioned, remind yourself that it's all about the work. With Jesus, you can say, "The Father is at work and I work, too."

POPE FRANCIS PRAYS

Work is part of God's loving plan,
we are called to cultivate and care for
all the goods of creation
and in this way share in the work of creation!
Work is fundamental to the dignity of a person.
Work anoints us with dignity, fills us with dignity,
makes us similar to God,
who has worked and still works, who always acts.

THURSDAY OF THE FOURTH WEEK OF LENT
Prayer Reinvigorates Us!
EXODUS 32:7–14; JOHN 5:31–47

A WORD FROM POPE FRANCIS

Prayer changes our hearts; it makes us understand better who our God truly is. It is important not to speak to God with empty words like the pagans. We need to tell him the truth: "But look, Lord, I have this problem in my family, with my son, with this or that…. What is to be done? You can't leave me like this!"

Sometimes prayer takes risks. Praying is also negotiating with God to obtain what I ask of the Lord…. The Bible says that Moses spoke to the Lord face-to-face, like a friend, and this is how prayer must be: free, insistent, with arguments, even reproving the Lord a little: "But you promised me this and you didn't do it!" Prayer is like speaking with a friend: in prayer one opens one's heart.

Following his face-to-face with God, Moses went down the mountain reinvigorated, saying, "I got to know the Lord better." And that strength allowed him to resume his work of leading the people to the Promised Land.

Taking the Word to Heart

One of the things most of us decide to do during the season of Lent is to pray more. We begin the season with a fresh new plan for improving our prayer lives. We might decide we're going to say the rosary every day or pray the Liturgy of the Hours. We might plan to go to daily Mass more often. We find a new prayer book and commit to using it at a set time during the day. These are all worthy goals, but as we come to the end of the fourth week of Lent, we have to admit that our intentions are often defeated by our inertia or simply by the day-to-day realities of life. Pope Francis reminds us that prayer is not about us and the things we do, it's about our relationship with God. He describes for us a very vivid image of talking to God as we would talk to a friend, a lover, a trusted confidante, a caring parent. He reminds us not to keep God at a distance, not to behave as though God doesn't know our innermost thoughts and feelings. Too often our prayer is what we think God wants to hear. And sometimes we do that to keep ourselves detached from our deepest needs as well. Sometimes it takes talking to a close friend to discover what's really bothering us. Pope Francis reminds us that God can be that close friend, as he was to Moses, to Abraham, to Noah, to Jesus, to all the saints through the ages.

Bringing the Word to Life

Set aside your formal prayers today and bring before God the deepest desires and fears that you hold close in your heart. Talk to God the way you would talk to your closest friend. And then take time to sit in silence with God. Let yourself be held in God's love, listening to the divine heartbeat in the world around you and in the depths of your own heart.

Pope Francis Prays

Lord, give us all grace,
for prayer is a grace
Teach us to pray as Moses prayed,
in freedom of spirit and with courage.
May the Holy Spirit,
who is always present in our prayer,
lead us along this path.

FRIDAY OF THE FOURTH WEEK OF LENT
The Kingdom Is Right Here
WISDOM 2:1A, 12–22; JOHN 7:1–2, 10, 25–30

A WORD FROM POPE FRANCIS

*E*ven today, Christians are persecuted. I dare say that perhaps there are as many or more martyrs now than in those early days. In some places, it's the death penalty, it's prison for having the Gospel in one's home, for teaching the Catechism. A Catholic from one of these countries told me that they cannot pray together—it's forbidden! They can only pray alone and in hiding. If they want to celebrate the Eucharist, they organize a birthday party, they pretend to celebrate a birthday and there they celebrate the Eucharist before the party. And if they see the police coming, they immediately hide everything and go on with the party, they hide behind cheer and good wishes. When these agents have left, they finish celebrating the Eucharist.

Never be afraid of persecution, of misunderstandings, even if because of them many things are lost. For the Christians, there will always be persecution, misunderstanding. But they have with them to face it the certainty that Jesus is Lord and this is the challenge and the cross of our faith. When this happens, in our community or in our heart, let us look to the Lord and think of this passage from the book of Wisdom that speaks of how the wicked beset the just.

TAKING THE WORD TO HEART

The pope's comments here remind me of stories from a priest friend who spent two weeks early in his priesthood filling in for a missionary priest in Saudi Arabia. Those stories from the mid-1980s now seem mild compared to news from the Middle East and Africa today. Too often what's missing from those stories on the evening news is the strong faith of those being martyred. We focus on the anger and the hatred being directed at innocent Christians, but we don't want to hear that they forgave their attackers. We want to respond with anger and vengeance. And yet, as Pope Francis reminds us, we follow the One who forgave his executioners as he was dying on the cross. We need to look beyond the suffering and remember that in the end, death doesn't have the final say. Our God always wins.

BRINGING THE WORD TO LIFE

Most of us will never experience this kind of persecution for our faith. On a visit to the San Sebastiano catacombs in Rome several years ago, I couldn't help but be struck by the felt knowledge of what the early Christians went through in order to celebrate Mass during the first centuries of the Church's existence. I felt a bit chagrined about the minor inconveniences I had complained about in the past. The next time you go to Mass, take a moment or two to give special thanks for the freedom to worship, the freedom to gather with others to pray. And say a prayer that one day everyone will know that freedom.

POPE FRANCIS PRAYS

Lord, give us the grace
to go forward on your path
and, if it happens, with the cross of persecution as well.

SATURDAY OF THE FOURTH WEEK OF LENT
Limitations
JEREMIAH 11:18–20; JOHN 7:40–53

A WORD FROM POPE FRANCIS

*I*nside the Church there are those who are persecuted from outside and persecuted from within. The saints themselves were persecuted. Many thinkers in the Church were also persecuted. I'm thinking of someone now, at this moment, not far from us, a man of goodwill, a true prophet, who in his books reproached the Church for falling away from the path of the Lord. He was immediately summoned, his books were placed on the index, they took away his platform, and this is how his life ended, not so long ago. Time passed and today he is a blessed. But how, one could object, how can he be a heretic yesterday and a blessed today? Yes, yesterday, those in power wanted to silence him because they didn't like what he had to say. Today, the Church who, thanks be to God, knows how to repent, says: no, this man is good! Even more, he is on the road to sainthood: he is a blessed.

TAKING THE WORD TO HEART

Pope Francis never hesitates to turn the light of truth inward as well as outward. Yesterday we were reminded of Christians who are persecuted for living their faith in predominantly non-Christian countries. But the Gospel, especially as John tells it, reminds us that Jesus suffered as much at the hands of those who shared his religious faith as he did at the hands of outsiders. Persecution happens because of misguided power, anger at perceived injustice, fear of those who are not like us, who don't share our beliefs and sometimes even our opinions. What begins as a disagreement over ideas can be magnified and escalated into rejection, ostracism, violence, and even death. And it can—and does—happen among Catholics of different philosophies, between Catholics and other Christians, between Christians and those of other faiths.

Bringing the Word to Life

In today's Gospel the Pharisees sneer at Nicodemus when they ask if he, too, is from Galilee, a rural region that the residents of Jerusalem considered backward and inferior. We do this even today. We think we know how people will behave based on what part of the country they're from. We divide our own cities and towns into good areas and bad areas. We absorb the prejudices of lifelong citizens even when we're new to an area. Often we wouldn't think of going to another part of town because of what we think we know about it, often based only on what we hear from others.

Spend some time today learning about another faith, another culture, another set of beliefs. Set aside as much as is humanly possible the division of us and them, me and other. Look at the world from someone else's perspective.

POPE FRANCIS PRAYS

O almighty and merciful God,
Lord of the universe and of history.
All that You have created is good
and your compassion for the mistakes of mankind
knows no limits.
We come to You today to ask You
to keep in peace the world and its people,
to keep far away from it the devastating wave of terrorism,
to restore friendship and instill in the hearts of your creatures
the gift of trust and of readiness to forgive.

SUNDAY OF THE FIFTH WEEK OF LENT
Embracing Death

YEAR A: EZEKIEL 37:12–14; PSALM 130:1–2, 3–4, 5–6, 7–8;
ROMANS 8:8–11; JOHN 11:1–45

YEAR B: JEREMIAH 31:31–34; PSALM 51: 3–4, 12–13, 14–15;
HEBREWS 5:7–9; JOHN 12:20–33

YEAR C: ISAIAH 43:16–21; PSALM 126:1–2A, 2B–3, 4–5, 6;
PHILIPPIANS 3:8–14; JOHN 8:1–11

A WORD FROM POPE FRANCIS

Christ is not resigned to the tombs that we have built for ourselves with our choice for evil and death, with our errors, with our sins. He is not resigned to this! He invites us, almost orders us, to come out of the tomb in which our sins have buried us. He calls us insistently to come out of the darkness of that prison in which we are enclosed, content with a false, selfish and mediocre life. "Come out!" he says to us, "Come out!" It is an invitation to true freedom, to allow ourselves to be seized by these words of Jesus who repeats them to each one of us today.... Our resurrection begins here: when we decide to obey Jesus's command by coming out into the light, into life; when the mask falls from our face—we are frequently masked by sin, the mask must fall off!—and we find again the courage of our original face, created in the image and likeness of God.

Jesus's act of raising Lazarus shows the extent to which the power of God's grace can go, and, thus, the extent of our conversion, our transformation. There is no limit to divine mercy which is offered to everyone! The Lord is always ready to remove the tombstone of our sins, which keeping us apart from him, the light of the living.

Taking the Word to Heart

Death always startles us with its suddenness, its finality. Even when a loved one has been sick for a long time and death comes as a release and relief for both the one suffering and those left behind, the initial reaction is one of shock and dismay. In cases of sudden, tragic, accidental death, this reaction is magnified. We who believe in the resurrection are no less likely to experience this very human reaction.

We see it differently at different times in our life. When we're young, death is an infrequent and scary interruption of life. When we're old, we sometimes feel like we've seen too much death over the course of a long life, and it seems almost unbearable in its familiarity.

Pope Francis today reminds us that the final death of our physical body is not the only death we suffer over the course of our lives. Sometimes you hear someone say of a loved one, "He was dead long before they buried his body." This can happen through tragic illnesses like Alzheimer's, stroke, or depression. It can also happen, as Pope Francis says, because of sin. Whatever we suffer from, Jesus is there to call us back to life.

Bringing the Word to Life

The promise of resurrection at the heart of our faith allows us to celebrate our loved ones even in their passing, because we know that life, not death, is the final reality. Give thanks today for those people dear to you who have passed from this world into the next, through the thin curtain of death.

Pope Francis Prays

May the Lord today,
give us all the grace
to rise from our sins,
to come out of our tombs;
with the voice of Jesus,
calling us to go out,
to go to Him.

MONDAY OF THE FIFTH WEEK OF LENT
Trusting When We Don't Understand
DANIEL 13:1–9, 15–17, 19–30, 33–62; JOHN 8:1–11

A WORD FROM POPE FRANCIS

We see so many dark valleys, so many disasters, so many people dying of hunger, from wars, so many disabled children, so many. The question spontaneously arises: "Where is the Lord? Where are you? Are you walking with me?" This is precisely Susanna's feeling, and today it is ours as well.

There is only one answer to this question. It cannot be explained. I am not capable. Why does a child suffer? I don't know; it's a mystery to me. The only thing that gives me some light—not to the mind, to the soul—is Jesus in Gethsemane: "Father, not this cup. But your will be done." Jesus entrusts himself to the Father's will; Jesus knows that all does not end with death or with anguish, and his last words on the Cross: "Father into your hands I entrust myself!" And thus he dies.

It is a true act of faith, entrusting myself to God who walks with me, who walks with my people, who walks with the Church. So perhaps I entrust myself by saying: "I don't know why this happens, but I entrust myself: You will know why." This is a grace. We have to ask for it: "Lord, teach me to entrust myself to your hands, to entrust myself to your guidance, even in brutal moments, in dark times, at the moment of death, I entrust myself to you for you never disappoint, you are faithful."

TAKING THE WORD TO HEART

The plight of Susanna in today's first reading is familiar to anyone who has been abused by someone with greater power, more authority, a high reputation in the community. The judges used their position to take advantage of someone with no power, no voice, seemingly no defense. In a similar way, the woman in our Gospel reading is brought before Jesus by those who are more interested in defending their authority than in treating her as a fellow human being. In each case, someone steps forward to defend the innocent, to raise up the oppressed, to speak for justice and righteousness.

But we know all too well that this doesn't always happen. Even in the Gospel, those who drifted away at Jesus's challenge returned to kill him and so reject his law of compassion. And so we come to the pope's words. Trusting God when we are suffering, when we are being treated unjustly, when we are abused goes against everything our human instincts tell us is right. We long for a Daniel to swoop in to vanquish the villains and save the day. We want a super hero. But the Gospel reminds us that what we have is in fact a savior, an advocate. But sometimes we have to wait for the plan to unfold fully.

Bringing the Word to Life

Call to mind an experience of injustice from your own life or the life of someone you love. Recall your response to the situation, your anger, your hopes, your fears. Take all of those feelings and offer them to God. Let your heart struggle to feel the faith and the trust that all will be well.

Pope Francis Prays

I entrust myself to you because you do not disappoint;
I do not understand, but even without understanding,
I entrust myself to your hands.

TUESDAY OF THE FIFTH WEEK OF LENT
The Sign of the Cross
NUMBERS 21:4–9; JOHN 8:21–30

A WORD FROM POPE FRANCIS

We must look at the crucifix and see this very mystery: a God emptied of his divinity?—completely!—in order to save us! From the cross Jesus lifts up all of us. For this reason the crucifix is not an ornament, it is not a work of art, with many precious stones. The crucifix is the mystery of God's annihilation, which he did out of love. In the desert, the serpent prophesies salvation. Indeed it is lifted up and whoever sees it is healed. But this salvation was not made with a magic wand by a god who makes things. It was made instead with the suffering of the Son of man, with the suffering of Jesus Christ. This is the history of our redemption, this is the history of God's love. This is why, if we want to know the love of God, we look at the crucifix.

TAKING THE WORD TO HEART

God tells Moses to make a bronze serpent, an image of the very thing that harmed the people. When they gaze on it, they will be healed. There's a deep truth to be found in confronting our wounds, trusting that in God's time and care the truth will bring healing. One place we might do that is before the cross that brought healing to the whole world.

Pope Francis reminds us that the cross isn't magic. Jesus's suffering was real. The brutality that inflicted the pain was an act of hatred and violence. This was no playacting by an untouchable god. Jesus knows what it is to suffer as wronged human being. And so we know that whenever, wherever we suffer, our God knows what we're experiencing. And we know that because he moved through it to the other side, we now have the hope that we will do the same. It can seem a fragile hope at times. Sometimes we only appreciate the fullness of truth when the pain is in the past. This season of Lent brings us to the foot of the cross so that we are once again reminded of the love and the mercy of God, who brings us hope in the midst of darkness, life out of the most seemingly hopeless death.

BRINGING THE WORD TO LIFE

If you have a crucifix in your home, take it down from the wall and spend some time in prayer reflecting on the mystery of a God willing to suffer for his people. If you don't have a crucifix, you might consider getting one. Sometimes a plain cross, without the image of the dying Christ, can allow us to forget the deep meaning behind the symbol.

POPE FRANCIS PRAYS

May the Lord grant us
the grace to understand
this mystery of the cross
a little better.

WEDNESDAY OF THE FIFTH WEEK OF LENT
Setting Others Free
DANIEL 3:14–20, 91–92, 95; JOHN 8:31–42

A WORD FROM POPE FRANCIS

*B*efore the spiritual and moral abysses of mankind, before the chasms that open up in hearts and provoke hatred and death, only an infinite mercy can bring us salvation. Only God can fill those chasms with his love, prevent us from falling into them and help us to continue our journey together towards the land of freedom and life.

The Lord, who suffered abandonment by his disciples, the burden of an unjust condemnation and shame of an ignominious death, now makes us sharers of his immortal life and enables us to see with his eyes of love and compassion those who hunger and thirst, strangers and prisoners, the marginalized and the outcast, the victims of oppression and violence. Our world is full of persons suffering in body and spirit, even as the daily news is full of stories of brutal crimes which often take place within homes, and large-scale armed conflicts which cause indescribable suffering to entire peoples.

Taking the Word to Heart

Stories of persecution from the Hebrew Scriptures were told and retold to give people hope in their own times of persecution. When we see on the news people being brutally murdered for their faith, we can get so caught up in the violence of the images that we lose sight of the faith of the victims. We miss seeing, as King Nebuchadnezzar did, one like a Son of Man giving them hope and rescuing them.

In John's Gospel, Jesus reminds his critics that their ancestor Abraham had great faith. And he tells them in no uncertain terms that God's truth will set them free. This truth is not always what we want to see or hear. It's not always going to be a promise fulfilled in this life. God's ways are not our ways, for which we should probably be grateful. In our time, we become impatient for answers. We need to remember that those answers will only come in God's time.

Today's reflection from Pope Francis reminds us that the hope of Lent is ultimately Easter and resurrection. But he knows that sometimes even the joy and hope of the liturgical seasons cannot entirely obliterate the darkness and violence of those who do evil in the world. And so his role and the role of the whole Church is to shine God's light into those places of darkness, to bring God's truth to those who offer only lies.

Bringing the Word to Life

This story asks us to think about the role our faith plays in difficult times. Lent can be a somber time for us, a time to let go of those habits that hold us back, those sins that separate us from one another. Sometimes we focus a bit too much on what we're going to do and what we need. Take some time today to reflect on others who are enduring great suffering. Find one thing you can do to help alleviate some of that suffering.

Pope Francis Prays

O God, Eternal Father,
in Your mercy hear our prayer
which we raise up to You amidst
the deafening noise and desperation of the world.
We turn to You with great hope,
full of trust in Your infinite Mercy.
We ask for the gift of peace.

THURSDAY OF THE FIFTH WEEK OF LENT
The Thread of Hope
GENESIS 17:3–9; JOHN 8:51–59

W) A WORD FROM POPE FRANCIS
When there is no human hope, there is this virtue which leads you forward. It is humble and simple, but it gives you joy, sometimes great joy, sometimes simply peace. We can always be certain that hope does not disappoint.

Hope is the humble virtue, the virtue that courses beneath the water of life, that keeps us from drowning in the many difficulties and losing the desire to find God, to find that marvelous face that we will all see one day. The same God who called Abraham and made him come down from his land without knowing where he should go is the same God who goes to the Cross in order to fulfill the promise that he made. He is the same God who in the fullness of time will make that promise a reality for all of us. What joins that first instance to this last moment is the thread of hope. Therefore, what joins my Christian life to our Christian life, from one moment to another, in order to always go forward—sinners, but forward—is hope. Yet, what gives us peace in the dark moments, in life's darkest moments, is always hope. Hope does not disappoint: it is always there, silent, humble, but strong.

Taking the Word to Heart

These powerful words from Pope Francis remind us that hope is one of three "theological virtues," along with faith and love. With St. Paul, we believe that the greatest of these is love, but hope is the virtue that keeps us going when even love seems to fail. Sometimes our ordinary use of the word *hope* can reduce it to something like wishful thinking: I hope I pass this exam. I hope my test results are good. I hope my children will be happy and successful. We use the word for things that are out of our control. We use it for times when perhaps our efforts have fallen short. We use it for all the uncertainties in our daily lives.

Pope Francis reminds us that the real source of our hope is always in God's faithfulness and mercy. Abraham has always been the prime example of this kind of hope. He left everything to follow God's call. We all have times in our lives when we, too, find ourselves going forth into the unknown darkness. In those times, hope in God's promise is all we have to cling to—and cling we must, sometimes with only our fingertips. The image of hope keeping us from drowning can seem all too real at times when we are overwhelmed by life's struggles: addiction, despair, depression, death.

The theme of our Lenten reflections is hope. The hope of Lent is clearly Easter and the resurrection. But there's a deeper hope that is with us each and every day, that knows no times or seasons. It's the ground on which we stand, the bedrock of our foundation. That thread of hope runs strong and resilient through our lives, caught at each end by the grace of God's merciful love.

BRINGING THE WORD TO LIFE

Write the phrase "I hope..." at the top of a sheet of paper and spend fifteen or twenty minutes free-writing your responses. Don't stop to think about or edit what you write. Let the Spirit move you from your surface desires to your heart's deepest hopes. Set the list aside for a day or two and then read through it, bringing those hopes to God in prayer.

POPE FRANCIS PRAYS

Our hope is in your hands.

O Lord, preserve our hope.

FRIDAY OF THE FIFTH WEEK OF LENT
Praising God
JEREMIAH 20:10–13; JOHN 10:31–42

A WORD FROM POPE FRANCIS

*I*f we are a little envious of one person or another, we don't contain our envy but sometimes share it with others by speaking badly about the person. This is how gossip seeks to grow and spread to another person and yet another. This is the way gossip works, and we have all been tempted to gossip. I too have been tempted to gossip! It is a daily temptation that begins slowly, like a trickle of water.

This is why we have to be careful when we feel something in our heart that would lead to destroying people, destroying reputations, destroying our lives, leading us into worldliness and sin. We must be careful because if we do not stop ourselves in time, that trickle of water, when it grows and spreads, will become a tidal wave that leads us to justify ourselves, just as the people from the day's Gospel justified themselves and eventually said of Jesus: "It is better that one man die for the people."

TAKING THE WORD TO HEART

The tension in the Gospel of John, even more than in the Gospels of Matthew, Mark, and Luke, is that from the beginning, Jesus is clearly the Messiah, the Christ, the Son of God. If all we have are the Synoptic Gospels, we can almost be persuaded that Jesus of Nazareth was a good and holy man who went about the countryside teaching people about God, healing their diseases, and preaching a moral lifestyle. In the Gospel of John, we have to wrestle with the fact that this good and holy man is in fact the human manifestation of the one, true God.

And yet, Pope Francis always finds a way of bringing lofty theology to a level where we can see clearly how it can have an impact on our everyday lives. One of his frequent themes, as we've seen even during this Lenten season, is the danger of gossip. Here he reminds us that our very tendency to dismiss it as a minor failing belies the danger it can have in disrupting relationships, social structures, and ultimately lives.

BRINGING THE WORD TO LIFE

We have opportunities every single day to say no to gossip. Find a way to pay attention to those opportunities for the next few days. You might want to keep a paper tally, a click of a counter app on your phone, moving a small item (a paperclip, a pebble, a dried bean) from one pocket to another. Just the act of noting these times may be enough of a reminder not to indulge in this seemingly minor sin.

POPE FRANCIS PRAYS

Let us ask the Lord to show us and the world
the beauty and fullness of this new life,
of being born of the Spirit,
of treating each other with kindness, with respect.
Let us ask for this grace for us all.

SATURDAY OF THE FIFTH WEEK OF LENT
Worldly Power
EZEKIEL 37:21–28; JOHN 11:45–57

A WORD FROM POPE FRANCIS

*T*hat is where the exercise of authority without respect for life, without justice, without mercy leads. And that is where the thirst for power leads: it becomes greed that wants to own everything. Mercy can heal wounds and can change history. Open your heart to mercy! Divine mercy is stronger than the sins of men.... We know its power, when we recall the coming of the Innocent Son of God who became man to destroy evil with his forgiveness. Jesus Christ is the true King, but his power is completely different. His throne is the Cross. He is not a king who kills, but on the contrary, who gives life. His going toward everyone, especially the weakest, vanquishes loneliness and the deadly fate to which sin leads. Jesus Christ, with his closeness and tenderness, leads sinners into the place of grace and pardon. This is the mercy of God.

TAKING THE WORD TO HEART

A toddler arguing with a parent will sometimes say, "When you're little and I'm big..." Even at that young age, they perceive that power has something to do with size and strength, even if they don't yet know the role that age and wisdom play. Sometimes we don't completely outgrow this immature reaction to power. If we don't have it, we want it. If we have it, we want to keep it. Power over another can become more important than power used for a good cause. When we're too long without power, we think only of turning the tables on those people who are keeping us from moving forward.

The religious leaders are convinced that Jesus is threatening their worldly power. "If we leave him alone, all will believe in him and the Romans will come and take away both our land and our nation." They fail to recognize or can't even imagine a world in which the passion, death, and resurrection of Jesus will have a truly cosmic significance in God's plan of salvation.

The scandal of the cross, even of the incarnation, is that God was willing to forsake all power in order to reverse the direction of humanity. In powerlessness freely accepted, Jesus modeled for us a new way of life, one that can disarm power when lived well. We've seen this throughout history in the lives of the saints and other courageous people willing to stand in the face of injustice and offer mercy and forgiveness. It doesn't discount the need for justice. Rather, a truly Christian response to violence and to power misused can break the cycle of revenge and violence.

BRINGING THE WORD TO LIFE

In what ways do we limit our awareness of God's design? How often do we imagine God's power in our warped human image, calling down vengeance and suffering on those who oppose us? Today take time to pray for someone whom you perceive as having unjust power. Ask God for genuine mercy for that person. Pay attention to how God touches your own attitudes in this exercise.

POPE FRANCIS PRAYS

May we exercise all forms of power
as service for God and for brothers and sisters,
with the criteria of love, of justice,
and of service to the common good.

PALM SUNDAY OF THE LORD'S PASSION
Who Am I?

PROCESSION GOSPEL: YEAR A: MATTHEW 21:1–11; YEAR B: MARK 11:1–10
OR JOHN 12:12–16; YEAR C: LUKE 19:28–40
FIRST READING, PSALM, SECOND READING: YEAR A, B, C: ISAIAH 50:4–7;
PSALM 22:8–9, 17–18, 19–20, 23–24; PHILIPPIANS 2:6–11
GOSPEL: YEAR A: MATTHEW 26:14—27:66; YEAR B: MARK 14:1—15:47;
YEAR C: LUKE 22:14—23:56

A WORD FROM POPE FRANCIS

We might well ask ourselves just one question: Who am I? Who am I, before my Lord? Who am I, before Jesus who enters Jerusalem amid the enthusiasm of the crowd? Am I ready to express my joy, to praise him? Or do I stand back? Who am I, before the suffering Jesus? … Am I like one of them? Where is my heart? Which of these persons am I like? May this question remain with us throughout the entire week.

Am I like Judas, who feigns loved and then kisses the Master in order to hand him over, to betray him? Am I a traitor?

Am I like Pilate? When I see that the situation is difficult, do I wash my hands and dodge my responsibility, allowing people to be condemned—or condemning them myself?

Am I like that crowd which was not sure whether they were at a religious meeting, a trial or a circus, and then chose Barabbas? For them it was all the same: it was more entertaining to humiliate Jesus.

Am I like the Cyrenean, who was returning from work, weary, yet was good enough to help the Lord carry his cross?

Am I like those fearless women, and like the mother of Jesus, who were there, and who suffered in silence?

TAKING THE WORD TO HEART

Pope Francis suggests an exercise that would have been familiar to St. Ignatius of Loyola. In his Spiritual Exercises, St. Ignatius uses the technique of placing oneself in a Gospel scene, imagining one's thoughts, feelings, and actions. As we begin Holy Week, we have the graced opportunity to be present once again at the passion and death of Jesus. But we are called to enter into the events, to be more than spectators.

As members of the body of Christ, we experience the death and resurrection that Jesus did. Everything in our lives—the heights of joy and triumph, the depths of suffering and death—is united with the life of Christ. The cross is before us now with its wordless challenge to love beyond death. Take some time this week to think about events in your own life that have given you an experience of Jesus's command to pick up your cross and follow him.

Bringing the Word to Life

Each time I hear one of the Passion narratives read, something different strikes me. I might notice a minor character or a bit of dialogue that makes a point I had missed in other years. Find an audio version of the Gospels online and set aside some time to listen to the Passion. Notice in particular the various characters in the story and think about Pope Francis's question, "Who am I?" You might be surprised by where the Spirit leads you this year.

Pope Francis Prays

Let us allow ourselves to be wrapped
in this mercy which comes to meet us;
and in these days,
as we keep our gaze fixed
on the passion and death of the Lord,
let us receive in our heart his boundless love
and in silence await the Resurrection.

MONDAY OF HOLY WEEK
True Concern for the Poor
ISAIAH 42:1–7; JOHN 12:1–11

A WORD FROM POPE FRANCIS

Selfishness leads nowhere and love frees. Those who are able to live their lives as a gift to give others will never be alone and will never experience the drama of the isolated conscience. Jesus says something remarkable to us: "Greater love has no man than this, that a man lay down his life for his friends." Love always takes this path: to give one's life. To live life as a gift, a gift to be given— not a treasure to be stored away. And Jesus lived it in this manner, as a gift. And if we live life as a gift, we do what Jesus wanted: "I appointed you that you should go and bear fruit." So, we must not burn out life with selfishness. Judas's attitude was contrary to the person who loves, for he never understood—poor thing— what a gift is. Judas was one of those people who does not act in altruism and who lives in his own world. On the contrary, when Mary Magdalene washed Jesus's feet with nard—very costly—it is a religious moment, a moment of thanksgiving, a moment of love.

Taking the Word to Heart

Judas's question in today's Gospel can generate nearly endless debate about the role of almsgiving and charity in the Christian life. The context of the story in John's Gospel reminds us that the message is always Jesus's identity as the Son of God.

Pope Francis refers to Judas as someone living in his own world. This can happen to us if we split off the various aspects of our life. If we separate our financial dealings from our spiritual lives, we lose sight of the things that really matter. We judge others by the size of their savings—or their debt—and not by the way they reach out to other to give or receive help. We would be scandalized, as Judas was, by the waste of money incurred by the anointing of Jesus. And like Judas, we would probably try to justify it by pointing to the good that could have been done with that money. But we would know in our hearts that the money wouldn't have gone to feed the poor either. We would have put it in a safe little investment fund "for a rainy day."

Bringing the Word to Life

On Holy Thursday many parishes take up collections of food or personal care items for those in need. Make a special trip to the store and buy nice items for this collection, things that you yourself would like to have. Too often we're guilty of giving old and unwanted items from the back of our pantries and closets for these causes. Reflect on the difference in attitude between Judas and Mary as you do so.

POPE FRANCIS PRAYS

We thank God,
who has raised up in many
a desire to be close to their neighbor
and to follow the law of charity
which is the heart of the Gospel.
But charity is even yet more authentic
and more incisive when it is lived in communion.
Charity is not merely about helping others,
but permeates the whole of life
and breaks down all those barriers of individualism
which prevent us from encountering one another.

Never Speak Poorly of Others
ISAIAH 49:1–6; JOHN 13:21–33, 36–38

A WORD FROM POPE FRANCIS

*J*esus was like a commodity; he was sold. He was sold at that moment and has also very frequently been sold in the market of history, in the market of life, in the market of our lives. When we opt for thirty pieces of silver, we set Jesus aside. When we visit an acquaintance and the conversation turns into gossip, into back-stabbing, the person at the center of our babbling becomes a commodity. I do not know why but there is some arcane pleasure in scandalmongering. We begin with kind words, but then comes the gossip. And we begin to tear the other person to pieces. And it is then that we must remember that every time we behave like this, we are doing what Judas did. When he went to the chief priests to sell Jesus, his heart was closed, he had no understanding, no love and no friendship. We think of and ask for forgiveness, because what we do to the other, to our friend, we do to Jesus. Because Jesus is in this friend.

Taking the Word to Heart

Reading the pope's words about Judas and the scandal of gossip has me imagining the whispers around the table at the Last Supper as Judas left their midst. John hints at what they thought Judas was about to do. In John's Gospel, Jesus knows what is happening at all times. The events are part of a greater plan. He knows that he will be betrayed, and he knows who his betrayer is. Yesterday we heard Judas challenge him over the jar of ointment used to anoint him. Today Jesus tells Judas to be about his errand. In both instances, John reminds his readers that Judas was the keeper of the community's money.

The danger of gossip is one of Pope Francis's favorite themes. It may seem an odd choice for Holy Week, but anyone who has worked in parish settings and helped with the Triduum liturgies knows that times of high stress can be a breeding ground for gossip and backbiting. Church people aren't immune from these common faults. One can only guess at the level of gossip Francis encountered in his first weeks in the Vatican as pope.

Bringing the Word to Life

Most of us aren't likely to betray anyone to a death squad. But as we meditate on the events of the Passion, we might reflect on the times we've betrayed a trust, the times we've talked about someone behind their back, the times we've stayed silent when a friend has been ridiculed. Resolve to keep silent when tempted to gossip and to speak out when others are gossiping. That sounds like a challenge, doesn't it? It is. Pray for the grace to meet it.

POPE FRANCIS PRAYS

Let us ask the Lord to show us and the world
the beauty and fullness of this new life,
of being born of the Spirit,
of treating each other with kindness, with respect.
Let us ask for this grace for us all.

WEDNESDAY OF HOLY WEEK
The Darkest Moment
Isaiah 50:4–9a; Matthew 26:14–25

A WORD FROM POPE FRANCIS

*W*hen all seems lost, when no one remains, for they will strike "the shepherd, and the sheep of the flock will be scattered" (Matthew 26:31), it is then that God intervenes with the power of his Resurrection. The Resurrection of Jesus is not the happy ending to a nice story, it is not the happy end of a film; rather, it is God the Father's intervention where human hope is shattered. At the moment when all seems to be lost, at the moment of suffering, when many people feel the need to get down from the Cross, it is the moment closest to the Resurrection. Night becomes darkest precisely before morning dawns, before the light dawns. In the darkest moment God intervenes and raises.

Jesus, who chose to pass by this way, calls us to follow him on his own path of humiliation. When at certain moments in life we fail to find any way out of our difficulties, when we sink in the thickest darkness, it is the moment of our total humiliation, the hour in which we experience that we are frail and are sinners. It is precisely then, at that moment, that we must not deny our failure but rather open ourselves trustingly to hope in God, as Jesus did. Dear brothers and sisters, this week it will do us good to take the crucifix in hand and kiss it many, many times and say: thank you Jesus, thank you Lord. So be it.

Taking the Word to Heart

As we get ready to enter into the Triduum, the sacred three days celebrating the passion, death, and resurrection of Jesus, it's good to recall that this isn't a dramatic recreation of these events. Pope Francis cautions that the resurrection isn't some kind of Hollywood happy ending. We know the truth of these events because of the way they continue to play out in our own lives. That said, the resurrection gives us real hope in our own dark moments and times of trial.

Bringing the Word to Life

Recall some of the difficult times in your own life and make a conscious effort to unite those memories with the passion, death, and resurrection of Jesus. This kind of offering doesn't take away the pain, but it gives it a meaning that it could not have when seen only from a limited human perspective.

POPE FRANCIS PRAYS

This week let us think deeply
about the suffering of Jesus
and let us say to ourselves: this is for my sake.
Even if I had been the only person in the world,
he would have done it. He did it for me.
Let us kiss the crucifix and say:
for my sake, thank you Jesus, for me.

HOLY THURSDAY
Actions Speak Louder than Words
EXODUS 12:1–8, 11–14; 1 CORINTHIANS 11:23–26; JOHN 13:1–5

A WORD FROM POPE FRANCIS

*J*ésus who serves, who washes feet.... He, who was the "master," washes the feet of others. An act. The second act: Judas who goes to Jesus's enemies, to those who do not want peace with Jesus, in order to take the money for which he betrayed him, thirty pieces of silver. Two acts. Today too, here, there are two acts: this one, all of us, together: Muslims, Hindus, Catholics, Copts, Evangelicals, but brothers and sisters, children of the same God, who want to live in peace, integrated. An act. Three days ago, an act of war, of destruction in a European city, by people who do not want to live in peace. But behind that act, as behind Judas, there were others. Behind Judas were those who paid money for Jesus to be delivered. Behind "that" act [in Brussels] are weapons producers and traffickers who want blood, not peace; who want war, not brotherhood.

Today, at this moment, as I perform the same act as Jesus by washing the feet of you twelve, we are all engaged in the act of brotherhood, and we are all saying: "We are diverse, we are different, we have different cultures and religions, but we are brothers and sisters and we want to live in peace." This is the act that I carry out with you. Each of us has a history on our shoulders, each of you has a history on your shoulders: so many crosses, so much pain, but also an open heart that wants brotherhood.

TAKING THE WORD TO HEART

Perhaps no action by Pope Francis has generated as much astonishment in the press (and perhaps in the Church!) as his washing the feet of prisoners—men, women, Christian, Muslim. A ritual that has at times become an honor for the elite once again returns to what Jesus intended: As I have done, so you must do. In his preaching on Holy Thursday, Pope Francis draws attention to the difference between the acts of Judas and Jesus at the Last Supper. The Holy Thursday liturgy is marked by the ritual gesture of the washing of the feet. We think of it as the institution of the Eucharist, and it is that as well. But the central action of service reminds us that our communion is more than a meal, more than nourishment for our bodies and souls. It's the act of taking on the mission, the ministry, the very body of Christ. And it is a challenge to us to remain in communion not only with one another, but with all people of the world. Our unity is far from perfect, but today's liturgy reminds us that if we are not always working toward that unity, then, like Judas, we are finding excuses to betray Christ's ideals.

Bringing the Word to Life

Today we enter into the holiest days of our Church year. We celebrate the passion, death, and resurrection of Jesus, the act that changed the very nature of human reality. Take some time to explore the way other religions similarly call their people to do loving acts of service for others. The more we know about those whose faith differs from ours, the more we will discover the common bonds that unite us.

Pope Francis Prays

Let us just remember
and show that it is beautiful
to live together as brothers and sisters,
with different cultures, religions and traditions:
we are all brothers and sisters!
And this is called peace and love.

GOOD FRIDAY
O Cross of Christ
ISAIAH 52:13—53:12; HEBREWS 4:14–16; 5:7–9; JOHN 18:1—19:42

O A WORD FROM POPE FRANCIS
Cross of Christ, symbol of divine love and of human injustice, icon of the supreme sacrifice for love and of boundless selfishness even unto madness, instrument of death and the way of Resurrection, sign of obedience and emblem of betrayal, the gallows of persecution and the banner of victory.

...

O Cross of Christ, image of love without end and way of the Resurrection, today too we see you in noble and upright persons who do good without seeking praise or admiration from others.

...

In you, Holy Cross, we see God who loves even to the end, and we see the hatred of those who want to dominate, that hatred which blinds the minds and hearts of those who prefer darkness to light.

O Cross of Christ, Arc of Noah that saved humanity from the flood of sin, save us from evil and from the Evil One. O Throne of David and seal of the divine and eternal Covenant, awaken us from the seduction of vanity! O cry of love, inspire in us a desire for God, for goodness and for light.

Taking the Word to Heart

The Passion According to St. John is always read on Good Friday. It gives us a perspective on the death of Jesus that reminds us that it wasn't simply a tragic occurrence in the life of a good man. It was the culmination of the earthly ministry of the Son of God, his hour of glorification, that moment when heaven and earth are joined and the life of Christ became the ongoing life of the Church.

Bringing the Word to Life

The longer reflection on the Cross by Pope Francis from which today's excerpt is taken offers a profound meditation for this feast of Good Friday. You might want to find it online and read through it slowly, meditating on all the ways the cross of Christ reveals itself in the world today. Ask God to show you how you might intercede for those who today carry the cross.

Pope Francis Prays

Dear friends,
let us bring to Christ's Cross
our joys, our sufferings and our failures.

There we will find a Heart
that is open to us and understands us,
forgives us, loves us
and calls us to bear this love in our lives,
to love each person, each brother and sister,
with the same love.

HOLY SATURDAY
Breaking Open Our Tombs
GENESIS 1:1—2:2; EXODUS 14:15—15:1 ROMANS 6:3–11; LUKE 24:1–12

A WORD FROM POPE FRANCIS

We, like Peter and the women, cannot discover life by being sad, bereft of hope. Let us not stay imprisoned within ourselves, but let us break open our sealed tombs to the Lord—each of us knows what they are—so that he may enter and grant us life. Let us give him the stones of our rancor and the boulders of our past, those heavy burdens of our weaknesses and falls. Christ wants to come and take us by the hand to bring us out of our anguish. This is the first stone to be moved aside this night: the lack of hope which imprisons us within ourselves. May the Lord free us from this trap, from being Christians without hope, who live as if the Lord were not risen, as if our problems were the center of our lives.

How can we strengthen our hope? The liturgy of this night offers some guidance. It teaches us to remember the works of God. The readings describe God's faithfulness, the history of his love towards us. The living word of God is able to involve us in this history of love, nourishing our hope and renewing our joy. The Gospel also reminds us of this: in order to kindle hope in the hearts of the women, the angel tells them: "Remember what [Jesus] told you" (v. 6). Remember the words of Jesus, remember all that he has done in our lives. Let us not forget his words and his works, otherwise we will lose hope and become "hopeless" Christians. Let us instead remember the Lord, his goodness and his life-giving words which have touched us. Let us remember them and make them ours, to be sentinels of the morning who know how to help others see the signs of the Risen Lord.

TAKING THE WORD TO HEART

As we come to the end of the Lenten season, we need to let ourselves feel the joy of new life. Sometimes it's hard to let go of Lent. We get comfortable with our penance, with the things we've given up. We like the feeling of self-imposed hardship a little too much perhaps. We also need to be challenged by the new life God may have planned for us. Just as Jesus came forth from the tomb, he calls us to open ourselves to new possibilities.

Pope Francis gets to the heart of our reluctance to celebrate the resurrection when he talks about our tendency to believe that our problems—or even the world's problems—are the center of our lives. Easter gives us a shift of focus, a way to let go of the darkness and embrace the light. All through Lent we've been looking for signs of hope. Easter reminds us that the greatest sign of hope for the human race is Christ's resurrection from the dead. Where he has gone, we cannot help but follow!

BRINGING THE WORD TO LIFE

The Easter Vigil may be the grandest experience of liturgy in the Catholic Church. Through readings and chant, psalms and hymns, we relive the entire story of God's covenant with us, from the story of creation through the Exodus of the Hebrew people, to the resurrection of Jesus and into our own lives. If you've never attended the Easter Vigil Mass, perhaps this is the year to try it.

POPE FRANCIS PRAYS

Christ is risen!
Let us open our hearts to hope and go forth.
May the memory of his works and his words
be the bright star which directs our steps
in the ways of faith
towards that Easter that will have no end.

EASTER SUNDAY
The Empty Tomb
Acts 10:34a, 37–43; Colossians 3:1–4 or
1 Corinthians 5:6b–8; John 20:1–9

A Word from Pope Francis

*L*ove has triumphed over hatred, life has conquered death, light has dispelled the darkness! Out of love for us, Jesus Christ stripped himself of his divine glory, emptied himself, took on the form of a slave and humbled himself even to death, death on a cross. For this reason God exalted him and made him Lord of the universe. Jesus is Lord! By his death and resurrection, Jesus shows everyone the way to life and happiness: this way is humility, which involves humiliation. This is the path which leads to glory.

The world proposes that we put ourselves forward at all costs, that we compete, that we prevail... But Christians, by the grace of Christ, dead and risen, are the seeds of another humanity, in which we seek to live in service to one another, not to be arrogant, but rather respectful and ready to help. This is not weakness, but true strength! Those who bear within them God's power, his love and his justice, do not need to employ violence; they speak and act with the power of truth, beauty and love. From the risen Lord we ask today the grace not to succumb to the pride which fuels violence and war, but to have the humble courage of pardon and peace.

TAKING THE WORD TO HEART

One of the ironies of the liturgical year is that we often find it easier to enter into the rigorous practices of Lent than to celebrate the joy of Easter and the Risen Lord. We know with our minds this great mystery of our faith. But we don't always experience that joy in our hearts. It goes so far beyond our human experience that we have nothing to compare to it.

At the heart of the story on Easter Sunday is the empty tomb. The stories of the appearances will come later, unfolding the mystery of the resurrection. But the first message to the apostles is that the tomb is empty. Somewhere in the darkness of the Easter Vigil and the pale dawn of Easter Sunday, each of us must confront the empty tomb and discover for ourselves the Risen Christ.

Pope Francis reminds us that our joy in the Risen Christ calls us to a quiet love and service, wrapped in the awareness that our life in Christ needs no trumpets or pomp and earthly glory. We have a peace in our hearts that is stronger than death itself. All our hope lies in that promise.

BRINGING THE WORD TO LIFE

In spite of all the displays of chocolate rabbits, egg dyes, Easter baskets, and spring flowers, today may be one of the last days when most stores are closed and people are free to spend time at home with family members. Enjoy the time together celebrating the promise of eternal life with loved ones living and dead.

POPE FRANCIS PRAYS

May there echo in your hearts,
in your families and communities
the announcement of the Resurrection,
along with the warm light of the presence of the Living Jesus:
a presence which brightens, comforts, forgives, gladdens.
Jesus conquered evil at the root:
he is the Door of Salvation, open wide
so that each person may find mercy.

MONDAY IN THE OCTAVE OF EASTER
Christ Our Hope Has Risen!
ACTS 2:14, 22–33; MATTHEW 28:8–15

A WORD FROM POPE FRANCIS

Life has conquered death. Mercy and Love have conquered sin! We need faith and hope in order to open ourselves to this new and marvelous horizon. And we know that faith and hope are gifts from God, and we need to ask for them: "Lord, grant me faith, grant me hope! I need them so much!"

The silent witness to the events of Jesus's Passion and Resurrection was Mary. She stood beside the Cross: she did not fold in the face of pain; her faith made her strong. In the broken heart of the Mother, the flame of hope was kept ever burning. Let us ask her to help us too to fully accept the Easter proclamation of the Resurrection, so as to embody it in the concreteness of our daily lives.

TAKING THE WORD TO HEART

The Gospels of Easter week unfold the mystery of the resurrection through those who were its first witnesses. In their words and in their actions we have a model for our own lives. The first reading, from the Acts of the Apostles, shows us how Peter and the others were inspired to speak out in ways that they never dreamed of before the resurrection. And Matthew's Gospel reminds us that from the beginning, there was opposition from those who felt threatened by this new movement of the Spirit.

Our day is not much different. Sometimes our faith moves us outward with great joy and fervent hope. But sometimes we need to go within, to renew our strength and our courage in quiet times of prayer. Depending on the circumstances of our lives this year, we might not be feeling the exuberant joy we expect in this season of Easter. Illness, death, unemployment, depression, and other human realities don't necessarily happen according to the liturgical year. But in a time when it seems the only constant is change, our faith—and even more, our hope—reminds us that God's love will always be there for us.

BRINGING THE WORD TO LIFE

The beauty of the liturgical seasons is that they offer us a new chance each year to experience the richness of God's work of salvation in our lives. Each year we grow a bit more in our faith. Each year the events in our lives offer us new insight into what the resurrection means for us and our loved ones. What one thing is different about your life this Easter?

POPE FRANCIS PRAYS

May the Virgin Mary
give us the faithful certitude
that every step suffered on our journey,
illuminated by the light of Easter,
will become a blessing and a joy
for us and for others,
especially for those suffering
because of selfishness and indifference.

TUESDAY IN THE EASTER OCTAVE
Carry the Light of the Risen One
ACTS 2:36-41; JOHN 20:11–18

A WORD FROM POPE FRANCIS

*T*he dominant sentiment that shines forth from the Gospel accounts of the resurrection is joy full of wonder, but a great wonder! Joy that comes from within! And in the liturgy we relive the state of mind of the disciples over the news which the women had brought: Jesus is Risen! We have seen him!

If only we were so luminous! But this is not just cosmetic! It comes from within, from a heart immersed in the source of this joy, like that of Mary Magdalene, who wept over the loss of her Lord and could hardly believe her eyes seeing him risen.

Whoever experiences this becomes a witness of the Resurrection, for in a certain sense he himself has risen, she herself has risen. He or she is then capable of carrying a "ray" of light of the Risen One into various situations: to those that are happy, making them more beautiful by preserving them from egoism; to those that are painful, bringing serenity and hope.

Taking the Word to Heart

One of Pope Francis's favorite distinctions is the difference between joy and mere happiness. This is something that's good to carry with us into the Easter season. His example of Mary Magdalene points to a key aspect of joy: It often follows a time of suffering, of disappointment, of struggle overcome and transformed. If Mary hadn't cared so much for Jesus, her sense of loss wouldn't have been as deep, but neither would her joy at their reunion. If we live our lives only on the surface, surrounding ourselves with acquaintances rather than real friends, we will find it difficult to experience deep emotions. Likewise, if our faith is only an intellectual exercise, a list of rules and doctrines instead of a personal encounter with the divine, we will miss the way it can truly change our hearts. One of the hallmarks of a true friend is someone who can accompany us through good times and bad, weeping and rejoicing as circumstances change. A genuine faith offers the same support. We are blessed if we have such friends, graced if we have such faith.

Bringing the Word to Life

Pope Francis reminds us that when we recognize the blessings in our lives, we will have a joy that we can share with others in good times and bad. If someone has done this for you recently, take a moment to let them know. As you reflect on your own joy in this Easter season, find a way to share it with someone who needs a ray or two of Christ's light in their lives.

POPE FRANCIS PRAYS

Let us allow this experience
which is inscribed in the Gospel
also to be imprinted in our hearts
and shine forth from our lives.
Let us allow the joyous wonder of Easter Sunday
to shine forth in our thoughts, glances,
behavior, gestures, and words.

WEDNESDAY IN THE EASTER OCTAVE
Take Up the Word of God
ACTS 3:1–10; LUKE 24:13–35

A WORD FROM POPE FRANCIS

The road to Emmaus thus becomes a symbol of our journey of faith: the Scriptures and the Eucharist are the indispensable elements for encountering the Lord. We too often go to Sunday Mass with our worries, difficulties and disappointments.... Life sometimes wounds us and we go away feeling sad, towards our "Emmaus," turning our backs on God's plan. We distance ourselves from God. But the Liturgy of the Word welcomes us: Jesus explains the Scriptures to us and rekindles in our hearts the warmth of faith and hope, and in Communion he gives us strength. The Word of God, the Eucharist.

Read a passage of the Gospel every day. Remember it well: read a passage from the Gospel every day, and on Sundays go to Communion, to receive Jesus. This is what happened to the disciples of Emmaus: they received the Word; they shared the breaking of bread and from feeling sad and defeated they became joyful.

Dear brothers and sisters, the Word of God and the Eucharist fill us with joy always. Remember it well! When you are sad, take up the Word of God. When you are down, take up the Word of God and go to Sunday Mass and receive Communion, to participate in the mystery of Jesus. There is always a Word of God that gives us guidance after we slip; and through our weariness and disappointments there is always a Bread that is broken that keeps us going on the journey.

Taking the Word to Heart

The story of Emmaus carries a depth of feeling that resonates with us because we've all experienced some level of disappointed hopes and dreams in our lives. Dreams jobs turn to daily drudgery. Failed relationships leave us brokenhearted. Illness and injury break our bodies and sometimes our spirits. If we're in the midst of such a time, the pope's words can sound hollow to our ears. And yet, if we heed them, we will discover the deeper truth to which they point. The Word of God can speak a word of hope and promise to our despair. The Bread of Life can fill an emptiness, a hunger, that gnaws at us. Sometimes all we have to do is show up. We have to make that much of an effort. Often we go with no expectations, almost no hope. And God surprises us with the right word, the right thought, a much-needed smile or hug from someone.

The message of Easter is that God shows up when we least expect it: a voice in the garden calling our name, a stranger on the road, a tap on the shoulder, breakfast on the beach or dinner after a long day at work. Sometimes the alleluias are quiet, but no less heartfelt for all that.

Bringing the Word to Life

Write out a few of your favorite Scripture passages. Make several copies and keep them in places where you will see them frequently. The more familiar we are with the Bible, the more it will nourish us when we most need it.

Pope Francis Prays

The Word of God, the Eucharist: they fill us with joy.
Through the intercession of Most Holy Mary,
let us pray that every Christian,
in reliving the experience of the disciples of Emmaus,
may rediscover the grace of the transforming encounter
with the Lord, with the Risen Lord,
who is with us always.

THURSDAY IN THE EASTER OCTAVE
No Fear of Joy
ACTS 3:11–26; LUKE 24:35–48

A WORD FROM POPE FRANCIS

We are afraid of joy. Jesus, by his resurrection, gives us joy: the joy of being Christians, the joy of following him closely, the joy of taking the road of the Beatitudes, the joy of being with him. Many times we are either startled when this joy comes to meet us, or we are full of fear: either we believe we are seeing a ghost, or we think that Jesus is a way of acting; indeed, we say we are Christians and we have to do it this way! Rather, we should ask ourselves: Do we speak with Jesus? Do we tell him: Jesus, I believe that you are alive, that you are risen, that you are close to me, that you will not abandon me? This is the dialogue with Jesus which is proper to the Christian life and is enlivened by the knowledge that Jesus is always with us, he is always with our problems, with our struggles and with our good works.

We need to overcome the fear of joy; we need to think of the many times that we are not joyful because we are afraid. In my homeland there is a saying that goes like this: when someone gets burned by boiling milk, he cries when he sees the cow. The disciples, who were burned by the drama of the cross, said: no, let's stop here! He is in heaven, that's excellent, he is risen, but may he not come back again because we can't handle it!

TAKING THE WORD TO HEART

On the surface, we might be tempted to scoff at the pope's claim that we're afraid of joy. But how often have we become so used to crisis and dread in our lives that we can't relax and enjoy a moment of peace, a time of no stress? How often do we manufacture a crisis just because we know how to solve a problem or fix something that's broken? Easter joy takes some getting used to. We love the rigors and the austerities of Lent. We're not as familiar or comfortable with the joy of Easter. One reason for this is that the kind of joy Jesus brings comes from living fully in the present. We are so much better at looking back to past pain or dreading the uncertainty of the future. Living in the present, the eternal now, requires both gratitude and grace.

BRINGING THE WORD TO LIFE

Do something today for no reason other than sheer enjoyment. It might be something you loved when you were younger. It might be something you've always wanted to try but were afraid of failing or looking silly. Prove to yourself that resurrection joy can be fully present in your life.

POPE FRANCIS PRAYS

May the Lord open our minds
and make us understand
that he is a living reality, that he has a body,
that he is with us and that he accompanies us,
that he has conquered:
let us ask the Lord for the grace not to be afraid of joy.

FRIDAY IN THE EASTER OCTAVE
Looking with New Eyes
ACTS 4:1–12; JOHN 21:1–14

A WORD FROM POPE FRANCIS

*S*ince Christ is resurrected, we can look with new eyes and a new heart at every event of our lives, even the most negative ones. Moments of darkness, of failure and even sin can be transformed and announce the beginning of a new path. When we have reached the lowest point of our misery and our weakness, the Risen Christ gives us the strength to rise again. If we entrust ourselves to him, his grace saves us! The Lord, Crucified and Risen, is the full revelation of mercy, present and working throughout history.

TAKING THE WORD TO HEART

The tricky thing about Easter is that while our faith and often our minds tell us that now life is all alleluias and rainbows, the reality is that sometimes we're still caught in some dark places. We might not be quite feeling the joy of resurrection. In today's Gospel, Peter, James, John and the other disciples are going back to their fishing boats. We get the sense that they've given up on this life of proclaiming the Good News. They're discouraged, they're confused. They've seen the Risen Christ in the upper room but then he vanished again. It turns out the fishing isn't all that great either. But they listened to the stranger on the beach telling them to try the other side of the boat. And Peter remembered the very beginning of his time with Jesus, when the novice told the experienced fisherman how to catch fish. He recognized the voice, the call, the inspiration. And, once again, his life was about to change.

Pope Francis reminds us that at the heart of it all—our joys, our sorrows, our trials, our challenges, our heartaches—God's presence is as simple and profound as a fire, a simple meal, a new way of seeing reality. The death and resurrection of Jesus reminds us that God knows it's never easy. The Risen Christ bore the wounds of the cross as a sign of that. Remember that he's with us every step of the way, loving us, nudging us forward, showing us a new way to see.

BRINGING THE WORD TO LIFE

Often when we struggle with some challenge in our lives—whether it's a situation, a relationship, or an internal issue—we close ourselves off from the very people who might be able to help. We go back to the old ways of coping that never worked all that well before. At those times, we may need someone to jolt us out of our inability to take a step or even see which way we need to go. But we're also the most likely in those times to reject anything new. Let the Easter season remind you to look for the positive opportunities, especially where there seems to be no way forward. You might want to find some image or object (for example, a boat, a fish, a bit of beach glass) to remind you of this Gospel reading when those times occur.

POPE FRANCIS PRAYS

O Cross of Christ,
teach us that the rising of the sun
is more powerful than the darkness of night.
O Cross of Christ,
teach us that the apparent victory of evil
vanishes before the empty tomb
and before the certainty of the resurrection
and the love of God
which nothing can defeat, obscure or weaken.
Amen!

SATURDAY IN THE EASTER OCTAVE
Strength to Carry on Living
Acts 4:13–21; Mark 16:9–15

A Word from Pope Francis

*I*n response to the order given by the head priests and Pharisees not to speak of Jesus, Peter and John stood firm in this faith saying, "We cannot but speak of what we have seen and heard." Their testimony reminds me of our faith. What is our faith like? Is it strong? Or is it at times a little like rosewater, a somewhat diluted faith? When problems arise are we brave like Peter or inclined to be lukewarm?

Peter teaches us that faith is not negotiable. We must get the better of the temptation to behave more or less "like everyone else." When we begin to cut faith down, to negotiate faith and more or less to sell it to the one who makes the best offer, we are setting out on the road of apostasy, of no fidelity to the Lord.

The very example of Peter and John helps us, gives us strength; as does the example of the martyrs in the Church's history. It is they who say, like Peter and John, "we cannot but speak." And this gives strength to us, whose faith is at times rather weak. It gives us the strength to carry on living with this faith we have received, this faith which is the gift that the Lord gives to all peoples.

Taking the Word to Heart

The journey of Lent is over. The journey of Easter has just begun. As we spend fifty days with the early Church, we have much to learn. The readings from the Acts of the Apostles are both inspiring and daunting. Questioned again and again by the religious authorities, Peter and John are steadfast in their conviction: "It is impossible for us not to speak about what we have seen and heard." For many of us, the problem is that the Good News doesn't always seem fresh and new. We've become too familiar with it. We hear the Word on Sunday, but we don't take time to reflect on what it means here and now. The stories from Acts refresh our awareness of what it must have been like to be that close to the earthly ministry of Jesus and his first apostles. But they also call to mind our own introduction to or embrace of that same faith.

Pope Francis reminds us that the temptation is strong to keep quiet about our beliefs, to blend in with the people around us. Whether through temperament, culture, or fear, we can be inclined to keep religion as a private matter. But when we do that, we start to lose hold of what we do believe. In a world where we're never challenged, it's easy to forget. This isn't to say we should go out looking for a fight, but as we look ahead to Pentecost, we might ask for just a bit more of the Spirit's fire in our life.

BRINGING THE WORD TO LIFE

Sometimes when we're wondering whether we have the faith of the apostles and martyrs, it helps to get back to basics. Spend some time today reflecting on the words of the creed. Find a copy of the Nicene Creed, the Apostles' Creed, or perhaps the formula used for the renewal of baptismal promises. Meditate on each section, asking yourself whether you really do believe it. Ask what difference that belief makes in your life. Ask what difference sharing that belief can make in the life of someone you know.

POPE FRANCIS PRAYS

Lord, thank you so much for my faith.

Preserve my faith, increase it.

May my faith be strong and courageous.

And help me in the moments when,

like Peter and John, I must make it public.

Give me the courage.

SECOND SUNDAY OF EASTER (DIVINE MERCY SUNDAY)
Hope Blossoms
ACTS 5:12–16; REVELATION 1:9–11A, 12–13, 17–19; JOHN 20:19–31

A WORD FROM POPE FRANCIS

So many people ask to be listened to and to be understood. The Gospel of mercy, to be proclaimed and written in our daily lives, seeks people with patient and open hearts, "good Samaritans" who understand compassion and silence before the mystery of each brother and sister. The Gospel of mercy requires generous and joyful servants, people who love freely without expecting anything in return.

"Peace be with you!" (John 20:21) is the greeting of Jesus to his disciples; this same peace awaits men and women of our own day.... It is a peace that does not divide but unites; it is a peace that does not abandon us but makes us feel listened to and loved; it is a peace that persists even in pain and enables hope to blossom. This peace, as on the day of Easter, is born ever anew by the forgiveness of God which calms our anxious hearts. ...In Christ, we are born to be instruments of reconciliation, to bring the Father's forgiveness to everyone, to reveal his loving face through concrete gestures of mercy.

Truly, God's mercy is forever; it never ends, it never runs out, it never gives up when faced with closed doors, and it never tires. In this forever we find strength in moments of trial and weakness because we are sure that God does not abandon us. He remains with us forever.

Taking the Word to Heart

The story of Thomas in the Upper Room is a clear example of Jesus meeting us in those wounded places in our lives and wordlessly offering us whatever we need to move beyond the hurt into a place of healing, trust, and peace. He doesn't scold Thomas for needing proof; he doesn't condemn him for a lack of faith. He holds out his hands and gives Thomas what he needs. We each have our own struggles with faith, with trust, with love, whether in our relationships with others, our connection to a church community, our responsibilities at home, at work, in school. As we place our needs before God's loving mercy, we open ourselves to receive whatever gesture of peace he offers us.

Mercy is the sign of God's ongoing presence in the world. Few people have made this more clear and compelling than Pope

Francis. And it's not just about realizing that God is merciful to us. It's realizing that we are now called, compelled, even commanded to be merciful to all those people we meet.

BRINGING THE WORD TO LIFE

In his preaching on mercy, Pope Francis often emphasizes the importance of listening compassionately to people who are wounded, struggling, searching for God's love. So often we want to rush in to fix other people's lives. The next time you feel this urge, take a step back and first simply listen to and love the person before you. God's peace passes all our human understanding. And often it lies beyond our limited human words.

POPE FRANCIS PRAYS

Let us give thanks for so great a love,
which we find impossible to grasp; it is immense!
Let us pray for the grace to never grow tired
of drawing from the well of the Father's mercy
and bringing it to the world.

SOURCES

Ash Wednesday: Holy Mass, Blessing and Imposition of Ashes, 5 March 2014

Thursday after Ash Wednesday: Morning Meditation in the Chapel of the Domus Sanctae Marthae, 19 February 2015

Friday after Ash Wednesday: Morning Meditation in the Chapel of the Domus Sanctae Marthae, 20 February 2015

Saturday after Ash Wednesday: Address of Pope Francis to the Parish Priests of the Diocese of Rome, Paul VI Hall, 6 March 2014

Sunday of the First Week of Lent: Most likely an Angelus excerpt

Monday of the First Week of Lent: Morning Meditation in the Chapel of the Domus Sanctae Marthae, 20 February 2015

Tuesday of the First Week of Lent: Morning Meditation in the Chapel of the Domus Sanctae Marthae, 1 March 2016

Wednesday of the First Week of Lent: Morning Meditation in the Chapel of the Domus Sanctae Marthae, 20 February 2015

The prayer for the Jubilee of Mercy

Thursday of the First Week of Lent: General Audience, Saint Peter's Square, 24 February 2016

Friday of the First Week of Lent: Morning Meditation in the Chapel of the Domus Sanctae Marthae, 9 June 2016

Saturday of the First Week of Lent: Doing the Unthinkable, Morning Meditation in the Chapel of the Domus Sanctae Marthae, 14 June 2016

Sunday of the Second Week of Lent: Ordinary and Extraordinary, Pastoral Visit to the Roman Parish of "Santa Maria Dell'Orazione, 16 March 2014; Angelus, Saint Peter's Square Second Sunday of Lent, 16 March 2014

Monday of the Second Week of Lent: Morning Meditation in the Chapel of the Domus Sanctae Marthae, 2 March 2015

Tuesday of the Second Week of Lent: Morning Meditation in the Chapel of the Domus Sanctae Marthae, 23 February 2016

Holiness Pope Francis to Participants in the Meeting Held in the Vatican on the Fifth Anniversary of the Earthquake in Haiti Saturday, 10 January 2015

Tuesday of Holy Week: Morning Meditation in the Chapel of the Domus Sanctae Marthae, 27 March 2013

Wednesday of Holy Week: General Audience, St. Peter's Square, 16 April 2014

Holy Thursday: Holy Thursday Mass of the Lord's Supper 2016

Good Friday: O Cross of Christ, from the Via Crucis in the Colosseum, March 25, 2016; Way of the Cross with the Young People, waterfront of Copacabana, Rio de Janeiro, 26 July 2013

Holy Saturday: Homily of his Holiness Pope Francis, Vatican Basilica Holy Saturday, 26 March 2016

Easter Sunday: The Empty Tomb, Urbi et Orbi Message of His Holiness Pope Francis, Easter 2015, central loggia of the Vatican Basilica, 5 April 2015

Monday in the Easter Octave: Christ our Hope Has Risen! Regina Caeli, Saint Peter's Square Easter, 28 March 2016

Tuesday in the Easter Octave: Regina Caeli, Saint Peter's Square Easter, 21 April 2014

Wednesday in the Easter Octave: Regina Caeli, Saint Peter's Square, 4 May 2014

Thursday in the Easter Octave: No Fear of Joy, Morning Meditation in the Chapel of the Domus Sanctae Marthae, 24 April 2014

Friday in the Easter Octave: From the Via Crucis in the Colosseum, March 25, 2016

Saturday in the Easter Octave: Strength to Carry on Living, April 6, in the Chapel of the Domus Sanctae Marthae

Second Sunday of Easter (Divine Mercy Sunday): Hope Blossoms, homily, Jubilee of Divine Mercy, Saint Peter's Square, April 3, 2016

About the Author

Diane M. Houdek is the author of *The Joy of Advent, Pope Francis and Our Call to Joy, Lent with St. Francis,* and Advent with St. Francis. She is a professed Secular Franciscan with a bachelor's degree in English and history from Marquette University and a master's degree in English literature from Northwestern University. She is the digital book editor for Franciscan Media and past editor of *Weekday Homily Helps* and *Bringing Home the Word.*